MW01088243

THE COLLEGE PRESS NIV COMMENTARY

PHILIPPIANS, COLOSSIANS & PHILEMON

THE
COLLEGE
PRESS
NIV
COMMENTARY

PHILIPPIANS
COLOSSIANS &
PHILEMON

ANTHONY L. ASH, Ph.D.

New Testament Series Co-Editors:

Jack Cottrell, Ph.D.
Cincinnati Bible Seminary

Tony Ash, Ph.D.
Abilene Christian University

COLLEGE PRESS
PUBLISHING COMPANY
Joplin, Missouri

Copyright © 1994
College Press Publishing Company
Second Printing 2000

Scripture taken from the HOLY BIBLE,
NEW INTERNATIONAL VERSION®.
NIV®. Copyright© 1973, 1978, 1984 by
International Bible Society. Used by
permission of Zondervan Publishing House.
All rights reserved.

Printed and Bound in the
United States of America
All Rights Reserved

Library of Congress Catalog Card Number: 93-743-1
International Standard Book Number: 978-0-89900-635-2

A WORD
FROM THE PUBLISHER

Years ago a movement was begun with the dream of uniting all Christians on the basis of a common purpose (world evangelism) under a common authority (the Word of God). The College Press NIV Commentary Series is a serious effort to join the scholarship of two branches of this unity movement so as to speak with one voice concerning the Word of God. Our desire is to provide a resource for your study of the New Testament that will benefit you whether you are preparing a Bible School lesson, a sermon, a college course or your own personal devotions. Today as we survey the wreckage of a broken world, we must turn again to the Lord and his Word, unite under his banner and communicate the life-giving message to those who are in desperate need. This is our purpose.

THE BOOK OF
PHILIPPIANS

INTRODUCTION

THE CITY

When Paul bypassed the seaport at Neapolis and moved eight miles inland to Philippi, he did so because Philippi, though small, was a city of some importance. The history of the city stretched back several centuries. A small village, known as Krenides, was captured by Philip of Macedon and annexed to his empire in 356 B.C. The area was attractive because of the many springs in the vicinity, and because of the nearby gold mines. Hence Philip named the city after himself, i.e., Philippi.

The city remained insignificant until conquered by the Romans almost two centuries later (168, 167 B.C.). The area was made a Roman province, and included in the first of the four districts into which the Romans divided Macedonia.

The most significant event of the pre-Pauline city took place in 42 B.C. There, on the plain of Philippi, the forces of Brutus and Cassius (Caesar's assassins) clashed with the armies of Antony and Octavian, only to go down in defeat. Thus Philippi was the spot at which the destiny of the Roman empire was set for some time to come.

Later (31 B.C.) Octavian defeated Antony. As a result of the battles of 42 and 31 B.C. a number of military veterans, from both the victors and the vanquished, were settled there. In 31 B.C. the name of the town was enhanced to honor Octavian (Caesar Augustus), its conqueror.

Philippi was made a Roman colony, a high privilege indeed for a provincial city within the empire. Rights of the citizenry included Roman citizenship, the right to own and transfer property, and exemption from certain taxes. The city was in municipal pattern and architecture modeled on Rome, as well as in legal and administrative detail. The citizens wore Roman dress, had coinage with Roman inscriptions, and used (though not exclusively) the Latin language. Roman citizens had certain rights under Roman law, a fact that stood to Paul's advantage when he came to Philippi (Acts 16:37ff).

The city was located on the Via Egnatia, one of the major Roman roads of the time. Some evidence indicates the road in this area was in bad condition during the time of Paul's visit, so that visitors to Philippi may have used the sea route (as Paul did) with greater frequency.[1] However, bad roads, though an inconvenience to travel, did not stop it completely. When Paul left the city it was by road toward the west.

Residents of the city would have included a core of veterans of the Roman wars or their descendants. Also in residence were Greeks, descendants of the native Thracian population, and some Jews. Some read the story of the conversion of Lydia in Acts 16 to indicate there were not enough male Jews in the city to constitute a synagogue. But others argue that there was a synagogue built by the river to which Paul went to preach.

ORIGINS OF THE CHURCH

The origins of this church are recorded in Acts 16:6-40. Compare the commentary by Dennis Gaertner in this series for detailed comments. The following should be noted.

First, it was by divine impulse that the mission to Philippi and Europe was undertaken. A vision, coupled with earlier prohibitions, spurred Paul on his way (Acts 16:6-10). Paul traveled with Silas, Timothy (who had joined the party earlier), and, by assumption, Luke, who is identified by "we" in

---

[1]Holland Hendrix, "Philippi," *The Anchor Bible Dictionary*, ed. David Noel Freedman (New York: Doubleday, 1992), 5:314.

Acts 16:10. This is based on the view that Acts was written by Luke. When Paul and Silas left the city, Luke was apparently left with the fledgling church, to be picked up by Paul when he passed through Philippi on his third journey (Acts 20:5).

Second, the initial convert in the city was Lydia (Acts 16:13-15), an open-minded God-fearer, whose profession (a dealer in purple cloth) and hospitality lead to the conclusion she was a person of some means. Though she is not mentioned in Philippians, two of the four specific names of Philippian Christians given in the letter are women, and it is generally thought that the women exercised significant roles in the church.

Third, a slave girl was exorcised, and this good deed destroyed her commercial advantage to her owners. In retaliation they inflamed a crowd, with the result that Paul and Silas were beaten and imprisoned in the most miserable of conditions (Acts 16:16-24).

Fourth, this incarceration served to make the faith of Paul and Silas shine more brightly, as they sang praises to God from their cell, rather than uttering the groans of pain that might have been expected. An earthquake so devastated the prison that the prisoner's cells were opened and their bonds loosed. The jailer, contemplating suicide because he thought his prisoners would have escaped, was reassured by Paul and Silas that they were all still there. More importantly, he found Christ, and he and his family became Christians in what is one of the remarkable conversions of the New Testament (Acts 16:23-34).

Finally, the release of Paul and Silas from prison and the embarrassment of the Philippian officials when they learned they had afflicted Roman citizens is told with a touch of humor. Paul and Silas, apparently taking their time, finally left the city, no doubt much to the relief of the city authorities (Acts 16:35-40). But their companion Luke stayed behind, with a group of believers whose ties to Paul through the years were especially affectionate. Though the first convert was a God-fearer, evidence indicates the church was composed predominantly of Gentiles who had not necessarily been sympathetic to Judaism. The date for these events is generally considered to be from A.D. 49-52.

PAUL'S LOCALE

Paul nowhere in this letter names the place of his imprisonment. A long held tradition, dating as early as the second century, identifies Rome as his locale. In recent years two other main options have been advanced: Ephesus and Caesarea. In considering this issue there are basic data to be kept in mind.

(1) Paul was a prisoner (1:7) and did not know the outcome of his trial (1:19f; 2:17).

(2) The place from which Paul wrote was also populated by those of "Caesar's household" (4:22).

(3) Timothy was with Paul (1:1; 2:19ff).

(4) The Christians in Paul's locale were engaged in evangelism (1:14ff).

(5) Paul hoped to visit Philippi if circumstances allowed (2:24).

(6) There was frequent communication between Philippi and Paul. The Philippians had heard Paul was in prison and sent Epaphroditus, who became ill. This news reached Philippi, and their anxiety reached back to Paul. The letter Paul wrote would be sent to Philippi, to be followed by visits from Timothy, and later (if possible) Paul himself (2:19-28).

A theoretical Ephesian imprisonment meets some of these criteria, but founders on others. Most telling is the fact that though Acts says Paul was in Ephesus for some time (Acts 19:8, 10) there is no record of an imprisonment there.

Paul was imprisoned for at least two years at Caesarea (Acts 24:27), but again that imprisonment does not account for all the statements in Philippians. One of the reasons for objection to Rome as the place of origin was that the distance between Rome and Philippi was too great for all the trips indicated by Philippians. But the distance was just as great to

Caesarea. Actually the journey from Rome to Philippi took about forty days. Thus a major objection to a Roman imprisonment, and justification for a Caesarean, is removed.

Two major objections to Rome have to do with the amount of time needed for travel, just discussed, and the change in Paul's travel plans from his announced intention to visit Spain (Rom 15:24, 29) to his intent to visit Philippi (Phil 1:25-27; 2:24).[2] Given Paul's unexpected changes in circumstances due to his arrest and imprisonment (Acts 21), a change of intent should not be found too surprising.

Though Rome cannot be proved to be the place from which Paul wrote, it does seem to fit the circumstances better than the alternatives. If from Rome, the date of writing was probably the early 60s. While holding this view, students still should not close themselves to evidence suggesting other possibilities. Despite the details in Acts and his biographical statements in the letters, there is still a great deal we do not know about Paul's activities.

REASONS FOR WRITING

Hawthorne lists a number of reasons Paul wrote this letter. From his list we may select the following as the most obvious.[3]

First, there was the matter of Epaphroditus and the gift sent to Paul by his hand. Paul wished to respond to their generosity (4:10-20). He also wished to allay their apprehensions about Epaphroditus (2:25-30), with whom he doubtless sent the letter.

Second, he took the opportunity to share certain news about himself and his situation. He especially told them of a problem he faced because some brethren hoped to create trouble for him by preaching Christ out of envy and rivalry (1:14-18). At the same time he addressed the issue of his imprisonment and his possible future (1:19-30; 2:24).

---

[2]See the comments on Philemon 22.
[3]Gerald Hawthorne, *Philippians* (Waco, TX: Word, 1983), pp. xlvii-xlviii.

Third, he wished to address a serious problem of division within the church. He names two women (4:2), but we suspect the problem was of wider dimension. There are touches throughout the book directed to this need, but it is addressed most powerfully in 2:1-11.

Fourth, Paul wished to warn about those he calls "dogs," "men who do evil," and "mutilators of the flesh" in 3:2. Later in the chapter he laments about "enemies of the cross" (v. 18).

EMPHASES

In addition to these central purposes there are certain notes sounded throughout the book which can enrich pursuit by the serious student. The joy motif through the book has been often observed (cf. the reference at 1:4). Though some have argued the church was a joyful one, we believe that not to have been the case. Paul's repeated exhortations indicate their lack of joy, and we suppose that a capturing of the "joy of the Lord" would go far to resolving the Philippians' problems.

Another noteworthy emphasis is the repeated use of the forms of the root φρον– (*phron*; references at 1:7). From examining these it can be discerned how Paul's call was for a whole approach to life, not just to superficial thought or action. Study of this term makes it clear that Christianity was a deep and total commitment to the Lord and to a way of life.

In addition the reader might examine the texts listed under "all" (1:1), "partnership" (1:5), and "in the Lord" (4:1).

DEVOTIONAL TEXTS

Some of the great devotional New Testament texts are found in Philippians (see 1:21; 2:5-11,12f; 3:7-11; 4:4-7,8f, and 11-13). Often these verses are taken out of context, and are given an independent existence. We note this to stress the fact that Paul did not write Philippians (or any letter) so it could be the subject of a commentary — though commentaries have real value. To follow Christ meant to live a life, not to judiciously make detailed observations about grammar, word meanings, syntax, etc. So if a commentary enhances understanding, that is a noble thing. But understanding may stop short of salvation. As Paul wrote to enhance discipleship, so this author hopes this work will have the same effect! To God be the glory!

OUTLINE

BIBLIOGRAPHY
PHILIPPIANS

Beare, F.W. *The Epistle to the Philippians*. London: Adam and Charles Black, 1959.

Bruce, F.F. *Philippians*. Peabody, MA: Hendrickson, 1983.

Craddock, Fred. *Philippians*. Atlanta: John Knox, 1985.

Harrell, Pat. *The Letter of Paul to the Philippians*. Austin: Sweet, 1969.

Hawthorne, Gerald. *Philippians*. Waco: Word Books, 1983.

Martin, Ralph. *Philippians*. Grand Rapids: Eerdmans, 1987.

Melick, Richard. *Philippians, Colossians, Philemon*. Nashville: Broadman, 1991.

O'Brien, Peter. *Philippians*. Grand Rapids: Eerdmans, 1991.

Saunders, Ernest. *First Thessalonians, Second Thessalonians, Philippians, Philemon*. Atlanta: John Knox, 1981.

PHILIPPIANS 1

SALUTATION (1:1-2)

¹**Paul and Timothy, servants of Christ Jesus,**
To all the saints in Christ Jesus at Philippi, together with
the overseersᵃ and deacons:
²**Grace and peace to you from God our Father and the**
Lord Jesus Christ.

ᵃ*1* Traditionally *bishops*

Though Paul was writing Scripture, he used the common
letter style of his day. The content, however, was far from the
same. It was enriched by the common experience of being "in
Christ" which he shared with his readers. We should not
expect here a carefully outlined document. It was a letter, and
as letters do, addressed a particular occasion without giving
exacting attention to the niceties of strict logical development.
But neither was the progress of Paul's thought haphazard.

1:1 Paul and Timothy,
Paul may well have suited the introductory self-descrip-
tions in his letters to the needs he addressed in those letters.
In some letters he called himself an apostle. But not here. His
apostolate was not in question in Philippi.

Paul joined Timothy with himself in the greeting. Timothy
was apparently part of the team which founded the Philippian
church (Acts 16:1-3,6,10; 17:14). Why was his name included
in this greeting? Certainly because he was with Paul and was
known to the Philippians. His name was also joined with

Paul's in the greetings in Second Corinthians, Colossians, First and Second Thessalonians, and Philemon. He was probably not Paul's scribe, as some have suggested, since he is mentioned in the third person in 2:19-23. For the same reason we know the letter was Paul's product, not Timothy's. If Timothy's name was included for other reasons, perhaps it was because Paul wished to enhance his status in view of his intention to send him to Philippi. Others think that inclusion of the name was to indicate Timothy's "amen" to Paul's words. It has also been suggested that Paul's use of "servants" as a mutual description of himself and Timothy was to show their equality. Thus Paul would not elevate himself by the title "apostle," since humility was the virtue which he would urge on the Philippians in the letter.

servants of Christ Jesus,

The word δοῦλοι (*douloi*) translated "servants" was the word normally used in the Greek world for slaves. The corresponding Hebrew term was used to refer to a person through whom God had acted (Moses in Num 12:7; the prophets in Jer 25:4; Ezek 38:17; Amos 3:7; and Zech 1:6). Thus some argue that Paul used the term to indicate that he and Timothy were God's instruments. This Hebrew sense is possible, but we prefer to understand the term in the Greek sense of slavery, as in 1 Corinthians 6:20 and 7:23, where Paul described the brethren as those "bought with a price." This seems to fit more neatly into the call for humility and unselfishness which is sounded often in this letter. Paul offered himself as a servant to the Philippians so that they could interpret his exhortations as "service" and not as "command." As Christ became a servant, so were they to become servants. Thus Paul opened the letter with a word that set the tone for what would follow.

To all the saints

It is noteworthy how often Paul uses the term "all" in this letter. One writer has suggested that it was sounded like the pealing of a bell (1:4,7,8,25; 2:17,26; and 4:21). Quite likely this language was used deliberately to reassure the church that no one was excluded from Paul's concern. He would not be accused of favoritism as he pleaded for unity.

"Saints" (ἅγιοι, *hagioi*) is the special term used for the recipients of this letter. Paul also employed the term in Romans 1:7; 1 Corinthians 1:2; 2 Corinthains 1:1; Ephesians 1:1; and Colossians 1:2. The basic idea of the word is to be "set apart." It draws its meaning from the Old Testament concept of the people of Israel being set apart because God chose them. In this unique relationship to God the Philippians enjoyed special privilege, as the letter will show. Further, they were also characterized by a particular lifestyle, as we will also see. These differences were obvious to the public, so that the followers of Christ became a visible element among the nonsaints in Philippi.

in Christ Jesus at Philippi,

Their special status was no human invention, but was made possible in Christ Jesus. Thus the cause of saintliness anticipates the greeting "grace" in verse 2. The expression "in Christ Jesus" and similar expressions such as "in Christ," "in the Lord," and "in the Lord Jesus" frequently punctuate this letter. If one searches for these occurrences, one is amazed at how central for Paul was the experience of relationship to Christ. This was no mere acquaintance, nor was it simply following the teaching of Jesus. It was a union with him, in which the saints shared Christ's resurrection life (3:9f). Though they were a special group in the city of Philippi, they were special there because they were first special "in Christ Jesus." These words indicate how extraordinary was the context in which this letter must be set.

together with the overseers and deacons:

Among the saints at Philippi were those called "overseers" and deacons. Some translations render "overseers" (ἐπίσκο-ποι, *episkopoi*) as "bishops," a term that derives from a transliteration of the word. This is the earliest literary reference to these groups to be found in Christian literature. This is also the only Pauline letter where these people were included in the address. Who were these overseers and deacons, and why did Paul mention them in his greetings only here? When we appeal to later New Testament writings we find the term for overseers employed in Acts 20:28 as well as in the climactic usage in 1 Peter 2:25. The basic idea in these texts is oversight, supervision, or protective care. In this case these ideas would have spiritual implications in terms of relationship to Christ. Though in later Christian writings overseers were involved with expenditures of money, when Paul mentions monetary gifts in Philippians 4:10-18, he does not mention them. It may be that in the providence of God oversight within the church ripened into more developed concepts found in 1 Timothy 3:1-7; Titus 1:5-8; 1 Peter 2:25 and 5:1-4. Here, in addition another church leader is mentioned in Philippians 4:3.

The term translated "deacons" (διάκονοι, *diakonoi*) simply means servant. (In fact, "deacon" is actually more of a translit-eration that a translation of the word's meaning.) Christians were often referred to in the New Testament by both the noun and verb forms of this word. First Timothy 3:8-10,12f gives qualifications of deacons who seem to have had a formal office in the church. They seem to have been special servants who operated in performing the tasks of the church under the supervision of the bishops.

Why did Paul address these groups specifically here? Some say he was responding to a letter the Philippians had sent him in which they were mentioned. Therefore he noted them in his response.

Others suggest that he wished the leaders to be foremost in recognizing Epaphroditus and receiving him properly when he came, and also in receiving Timothy (2:19-30). He may have wished the cooperation of these leaders in dealing with the Philippian problems addressed in the letter. If that was the case, however, it is puzzling why Paul did not mention such leaders in his other letters. It is possible that the Philip-pian church was the first to have appointed individuals to these positions.

We should also note that the term "overseers" is plural. There was no single bishop (overseer) in the church at this point.

1:2 Grace and peace to you

The term "grace" (χάρις, *charis*) is similar in form to the usual Greek greeting χαῖρε (*chaire*), "hail," but this subtle change in meaning catches up the essence of what it means to be a follower of Jesus. Everything is from God, and because grace has been given from God, peace is possible. "Peace" (εἰρήνη, *eirēnē*) was also frequently used in Paul's greetings. It implies health, well-being, and prosperity. When properly understood, these were blessings of following Jesus and of being of God's special race of people. Thus, as God had given him grace and peace, so now Paul blessed others with the same gifts. But he recognized that he could offer them only because they had been offered by God in Christ.

from God our Father and the Lord Jesus Christ.

Jesus had taught his followers the special dimensions of the fatherhood of God. Note especially the use of the term in Luke 11:2,13. Therefore as God's sons through Christ they could address him as "Father."

To address Jesus as "Lord" was to recognize his sovereignty and equality with God, as God was Lord. It was also to recognize his role as Messiah. The theme of Lordship becomes particularly pointed in 2:9-11.

I. THANKSGIVING AND PRAYER (1:3-11)

A. THANKSGIVING (1:3-8)

³I thank my God every time I remember you. ⁴In all my prayers for all of you, I always pray with joy ⁵because of your partnership in the gospel from the first day until now, ⁶being confident of this, that he who began a good work in

you will carry it on to completion until the day of Christ Jesus.

[7]It is right for me to feel this way about all of you, since I have you in my heart; for whether I am in chains or defending and confirming the gospel, all of you share in God's grace with me. [8]God can testify how I long for all of you with the affection of Christ Jesus.

Letters of Paul's day often included a section which could have one or more basic functions. It could be an expression of thanksgiving, or a prayer to the gods in whom the writer believed. It might include some favorable reference to the recipients of the letter, as best wishes or a prayer for them. There may have been something about the circumstances of the writer. Paul has taken this section of the normal letter and expanded it. Normally the themes that were touched were those that were expanded and developed later in the letter. Thus in verses 3 and following we will see many ideas that were important in Paul's mind as he wrote.

Verses 3-6 are centered in remembrance; that is, in Paul's past experience with the Philippians. In verse 7, as he had done briefly in verse 3, Paul indicates his present attitude as he writes. In verses 9-11 Paul prays that God will bless his readers in the future.

He begins by thanking God for them. Before he will finish this section, we will learn that Paul was thankful because they had remembered him and thus been his partners; and he was thankful because he was confident that God would complete the good work in them which he had begun. There is then in these verses a sense of confidence in the power of prayer. Paul was not merely extending good wishes, but believed that God would work in their lives.

1:3 I thank my God

There is an intimacy in the expression "my God" — an expression found elsewhere in Romans 1:8 and Philemon 4. Paul recognized that the goodness of the Philippians was due to God's work in them, and not to their natural graciousness.

every time I remember you.
Some have argued that a legitimate translation of the Greek μνείᾳ ὑμῶν (*mneia hymōn*, literally "remembrance of you") rendered "I remember you" could be "you remember me." If that translation were accepted it could refer to the gifts they had sent Paul (4:10-18) as well as to other ways in which the Philippians had cared for him. Both translations reflect concepts found in the letter, and which are Christian. It is difficult to know which to accept here.

Verses 3 and 4 seem to indicate a regular regimen of prayer on Paul's part. We would say that the Philippians were on Paul's "prayer list."

1:4 In all my prayers for all of you,
Here, as in verse 1, Paul mentions "all" the Christians at Philippi. Again he wished to indicate that none were omitted. This would be an appropriate response to any division in the church which would separate Christians from one another. Paul was not going to take sides and exclude some.

I always pray with joy
The joy theme is here first introduced in the letter. It will be sounded again and again. References are found in 1:18, 25; 2:2,17,18,28,29; 3:1; and 4:1,4,10. The noun form of the word (χαρά, *chara*) is found five times and the verb form (χαίρω, *chairō*) is found eleven times in Philippians. Paul speaks of more than just a mood. This is a deep confidence that was rooted in God's sovereign control of the universe and the assurance of ultimate victory for those in Christ. Emotional fluctuations would not trouble this source of joy. Note Paul's statement of this confidence in 3:20. Statements of joy are significant given the fact that Paul was in prison. But imprisonment did not diminish his joy because that joy was grounded in something deeper.

Paul prayed for the Philippians as they prayed for him (1:19). The word for prayer here is not Paul's usual term, but indicates a specific need that was carried to God. The content of the prayer, however, is not given until verse 9, after Paul has spoken of his relationship to the Philippians and his feelings for them.

1:5 because of your partnership in the gospel

Paul's relations with the Philippians had been special through the years. The term "partnership" is the Greek κοι-νωνία (*koinōnia*), used by Paul in thirteen of the nineteen New Testament usages. In Philippians it occurs in 1:7; 2:1; 3:10 and 4:15, besides the present text. It has a broad realm of significance, and certainly would include here the financial help they had sent (4:10-18). We know that Paul was sent help in Thessalonica more than once (Phil 4:16); that help was sent once to him in Corinth (2 Cor 11:9); and now help had been sent to him as he was in prison. But, beyond financial help, the larger sense of partnership here seems to be sharing in the gospel, or in the life in Christ.

from the first day until now,

This partnership took place "from the first day." Meanings of the term "first day" range from the suggestion that it meant the beginning of Paul's evangelism in Philippi, to that it was the beginning of his evangelism after leaving Philippi, to that it was the beginning of the European mission. These conjectures may be overworking the point. Paul may simply have been saying that the Philippians, in all the time of their acquaintance, had shared with him in the work of the Lord.

1:6 being confident of this, that he who began a good work in you will carry it on to completion

Now Paul moves from the past to the future, expressing confidence in the work that God would do in the lives of the Philippians. His confidence was not merely humanistic, but was based in the very nature of God. God, if men would allow it, would complete the work that he does in human lives. Though the "good work" could include financial help given Paul, it seems likely, from the nature of this verse, that it embraced more than that, i.e., embraced the entire experience of living in Christ. There was need for perseverance in this endeavor, but there was also the expectation of increased growth and experienced richness in relationship to Christ. Paul's prayer suggests a prayer that all Christians would do well to employ.

until the day of Christ Jesus.

The "day of Christ Jesus" is understood as the day of his return. It is possible to read these words in a way that implies an expectation that this event would occur soon. There is no doubt that the early Christians expected the Lord to return at any time, though the exact time was unknown. The passage of the centuries has dimmed the modern church's expectation of the Lord's return. It might be well if the church could recapture the sense of an event which could at any time break into history.

1:7 It is right for me to feel this way about all of you,

Although the term "it is right," which was Paul's affirmation that he had the Philippians in his heart, may seem defensive, as if Paul were criticized for his prayers, actually he was choosing a strong way to indicate how deep his feelings were. Verses 7 and 8 are characterized by strong emotion, and show in a beautiful way the relationship between the church and the prisoner. Paul's days in prison were brightened by the contemplation of these brothers and sisters.

The word "feel" translates an important Greek term (φρονεῖν, *phronein*). Philippians contains one third of its New Testament usages (2:2 [twice], 5; 3:15 [twice], 16 [variant], 19; 4:2, 10 [twice].) The basic idea conveyed by the word was a frame of mind, or a life direction. The sense is of thought, but there are emotional overtones. It is a mistake, however, to interpret the term simply as an emotion.

It is often easy to feel deeply for one segment of a group and not for another, but Paul by using "all" made it clear that this passionate language excluded none of those in the Philippian church. Note the same term in verses 1 and 4. So Paul knew about these people, but also cared deeply about them.

since I have you in my heart;

Some translations render the Greek behind "since I have you in my heart" as "you hold me in your heart." Both renderings are possible from the Greek and commentators are divided. We believe, on the basis of verse eight, that the reading of the NIV makes better sense here.

for whether I am in chains or defending and confirming the gospel,

Defending and confirming the gospel are part of the same experience, since only one article is used with the two terms, indicating that they were one thing. These were legal terms, and probably referred to Paul's coming trial, though other opinions have been offered.

all of you share in God's grace with me.

In these traumatic times Paul was comforted by a sense of God's grace, but was also comforted by the realization that others shared in that grace. He was not alone, but was part of a supportive community, which, though not with him in person, was involved with him in prayer. One author has suggested that the church might be described as "sharers in God's grace."

1:8 God can testify how I long for all of you with the affection of Christ Jesus.

Paul continued expressing his deep attachment to his readers in this verse by calling God to testify to his longing for them. If they could not see Paul's heart, God could. So in this serious way he affirmed his concern for them. Though he had affection for them, the sense was intensified by reference to the affection of Jesus. Paul might have spoken of "my affection," but the passage as it reads makes the statement more powerful. Any understanding of Christ would have to begin with a sense of Jesus' deep affection and compassion. To describe affection in that way was to describe it as powerfully as possible. Paul may have expressed himself this way in the event any doubted the sincerity of his words. To invoke the names of God and Christ when a statement of love was made falsely would be a terrible thing indeed.

B. PRAYER FOR LOVE GROWING TOWARD GLORY (1:9-11)

⁹And this is my prayer: that your love may abound more and more in knowledge and depth of insight, ¹⁰so that you may be able to discern what is best and may be pure and blameless until the day of Christ, ¹¹filled with the fruit of righteousness that comes through Jesus Christ — to the glory and praise of God.

We come now to the prayer to which reference was made in verses 3 and 4. Just as verse 6 had expressed confidence for the readers' Christian growth until the day of Christ, now in verses 9-11 the same thought is repeated, keeping in mind the ultimate return of the Lord (v. 10).

1:9 And this is my prayer:
The word for prayer here is the broader term (προσεύχομαι, *proseuchomai*) contrasted to the narrower term found in verse 4, which there indicated a more specific petition. The content of the prayer was for love, but love defined in the very specific ways the context indicates. The result of this love was that the quality of life would be such that God would be glorified.

that your love may abound more and more in knowledge and depth of insight,
There were two things for which Paul prayed. The first was

love that was abounding and able to discern. Secondly, he prayed for their character, that they might be pure and blameless. The love for which he prayed could be love for God, but in context it seems more appropriately to indicate love for others. The need for this love would become obvious as the letter progressed, and as Paul discussed the need for the church to seek unity. This love, which was enhanced through prayer, was not simply a feeling, but on the other hand neither was it just a bookish kind of knowledge. Genuine love would produce moral insight and thus appropriate action. One commentator has even suggested that Paul was combatting an "enthusiastic" love which needed to be tempered and guided by knowledge and insight.

Paul prayed that this love would abound, which implied it would be overflowing. As one has said, there was to be so much love there would be no room to store it. The new age of men in Christ was to be marked by this remarkable excess of love, characterized by knowledge and insight. It was not an easy tolerance of any belief or manner of life. Love would weigh matters in view of the deeper purposes of God, and thus make decisions and carry them into action.

1:10 so that you may be able to discern what is best and may be pure and blameless until the day of Christ,

To "be able to discern what is best," as this verse indicates, required that some things would be rejected by love as not being best. Love was therefore a thinking thing, which, like wisdom, observed, and sifted, and decided. There may be many ways to make decisions, but Paul prayed that their way would be the highest; the way of love. Thus the pure and blameless quality of life came through prayer, as did the righteousness indicated in the next verse. The pure person was one who was sincere and honest and whose mind was not polluted by those things which did not come from God. The basic idea of "blameless" (ἀπρόσκοποι, *aproskopoi*) seems to relate to the idea of stumbling; either not causing others to stumble, or not stumbling oneself. As in verse 6 there was a reference to the day of Christ, so again this end of time reality is noted as the goal and climax of Christian striving.

1:11 filled with the fruit of righteousness that comes through Jesus Christ —

The theme of personal integrity continues here, with the expression "fruit of righteousness" (καρπὸν δικαιοσύνης, *karpon dikaiosynēs*). This could mean either righteousness which was itself the fruit (like an orchard), or it could mean that righteousness within one produced the right kind of fruit. Here it was not the sinlessness which was given because of what Christ had done, but it was a moral quality. Consonant with the idea that prayer produces righteousness, here Paul said it came through Jesus Christ.

to the glory and praise of God.

The conclusion, or doxology, of this section is the expression "to the glory and praise of God." Paul has not been discussing human achievement, but that which comes as the result of prayer and God's intercession. It was not how good humans had been, but rather how good and gracious God has been.

II. PAUL'S SITUATION AND ATTITUDE (1:12-26)

A. THE INFLUENCE OF PAUL'S CHAINS (1:12-14)

[12]**Now I want you to know, brothers, that what has happened to me has really served to advance the gospel. [13]As a result, it has become clear throughout the whole palace guard[a] and to everyone else that I am in chains for Christ. [14]Because of my chains, most of the brothers in the Lord have been encouraged to speak the word of God more courageously and fearlessly.**

[a]*13* Or *whole palace*

In verses 12-14 Paul reassured the brothers that his experiences had advanced the gospel. Consequently the palace guard and all others knew that his chains were for Christ. And the Christians had been encouraged to speak God's word with greater courage.

The form of Philippians differs from some of Paul's other letters in that he intersperses biographical material with instruction and exhortation. Even the biography, however, has an instructive purpose. Verses 12-26 comprise this first biographical section. The two others are 2:19–3:14 and 4:10-20. Though Paul speaks about himself, verses 12-18 seem to be more basically about the preaching of Christ. In verse 14 it is mentioned specifically, and verses 15-18 describe an unusual situation which Paul resolved by rejoicing that regardless of motives Christ was preached. As one author has said the picture is not so much a Pauline self-portrait, as one of the gospel's progress.

1:12 Now I want you to know, brothers,

The words "I want you to know" may have implied an inquiry by the Philippians, or may indicate that people would expect the opposite result from the one Paul now announced. His language may imply the expectation that his circumstances would hinder the gospel. He made it clear that the opposite had occurred. This had two results. First, (v. 13) his guard and "everyone else" had further understanding of his circumstances, centering in the knowledge of Christ. Second, most of the brothers had been emboldened by Paul's circumstances to overcome any reticence to speak God's word.

Some have even suggested (though the text does not hint at it) that Paul may have been responding to those who might argue that if God were really with him, he would not have allowed Paul to be imprisoned.

that what has happened to me

As Paul had prayed for deepened knowledge to characterize the Philippians (v. 9), so now he advances their knowledge of his situation. He calls his state "what has happened to me." This may have referred to his imprisonment and its consequences. But it is also possible that it referred to some subsequent episode, perhaps even that mentioned in verses 15-18. The Greek expression is literally "my affairs." This is so general that we cannot exactly define Paul's situation. Whatever it was, it was assumed that it might harm the cause of Christ.

has really served to advance the gospel.

The word "advance" (προκοπή, *prokopē*) commonly described the removing of obstacles, as might be done before an advancing army. Here a circumstance that might have appeared to be an obstacle really had the opposite result.

1:13 As a result, it has become clear

It would appear that either ignorance or misconception had once characterized what people knew of Paul's imprisonment, but no longer. One would assume from "it has become clear" that the gospel had become quite a topic of conversation. One might also assume, knowing Paul, that he had not been passive during his imprisonment.

throughout the whole palace guard

"Palace guard" (πραιτώριον, *praitōrion*) was an expression which originally designated a leader's tent in a Roman camp, then later the official residence of the governor in a Roman palace. It is generally held, however, that in this context the reference was not to a location, but to soldiers. The next expression indicates individuals ("everyone else") and this would imply that "palace guard" also indicates individuals.

and to everyone else

"Everyone else" may have been others concerned with the disposition of Paul's case. Since the term is general, it could extend even beyond that. This prisoner was not hidden away in anonymity.

that I am in chains for Christ.

Why was Paul initially imprisoned? Was it assumed that he was a political prisoner? If so, that assumption had now been placed aside. He was in prison for Christ. Does this suggest that his jailers considered that was a legitimate grounds for incarceration, or that it was not a legitimate reason and they were not aware of it? Perhaps these questions are not the major interest in the text. Most important was that Christ was now known through Paul and his circumstances. In a sense it could be said that Paul was acknowledging a higher imprisoning authority than Rome; that he was indeed God's prisoner.

Yet it is tantalizing to know exactly how and why Paul was imprisoned. If a Roman imprisonment is assumed the narrative in Acts still leaves the reader with some dissatisfaction as to any solid legal reason for Paul's presence in jail. The expression "in Christ," nonetheless, must indicate the imprisonment had something to do with Paul's Christian activity. In 3:10 he speaks of himself as a sharer in Christ's sufferings.

1:14 Because of my chains, most of the brothers

Now Paul "moves out" of prison, to consider the brothers. Behind his words we sense reticence, perhaps even embarrassment, on the part of the brothers, reluctant to preach because of danger or humiliation. If there was danger, Paul's circumstances had emboldened them to rise above it. Boldness and shame in Philippi are noted in verse 20. Apparently both in Paul's location and in Philippi the problem of reticence in proclamation and discipleship occurred.

The word "most" is intriguing. Were there brethren who, despite Paul, still held back from proclamation? Perhaps shyness to preach the word is a problem with which the church must always deal.

in the Lord have been encouraged to speak the word of God more courageously and fearlessly.

The expression "in the Lord" (ἐν κυρίῳ, en kyriō) in the NIV modifies "brothers." Some feel this is unnecessarily repetitive and note that the Greek could just as well use the words to modify "encourage"; i.e., the brothers are encouraged in the Lord. This might imply that God had given them supernatural help, likely in response to prayer, leading them to overcome reluctance in evangelism. We can conjecture the circumstances. Some might have asked, when learning that Paul was in prison for Christ, what it was about Christ that would lead a person to accept jail. This might have opened up preaching opportunities for the brethren. Or his circumstances might have demonstrated that prison was not that tragic, or that if one followed Christ, prison did not matter. They may have thought that if Paul had such courage, so should they.

B. OPPOSITE MOTIVES FOR PREACHING CHRIST (1:15-18a)

[15]It is true that some preach Christ out of envy and rivalry, but others out of goodwill. [16]The latter do so in love, knowing that I am put here for the defense of the gospel. [17]The former preach Christ out of selfish ambition, not sincerely, supposing that they can stir up trouble for me while I am in chains.[a] [18]But what does it matter? The important thing is that in every way, whether from false motives or true, Christ is preached. And because of this I rejoice.

[a]*16, 17* **Some late manuscripts have verses 16 and 17 in reverse order.**

Those who preached Christ did so from two motives. Some who did so out of envy and rivalry, selfish ambition and insincerity hoped to create trouble for Paul (vv. 15,17). Others preached out of love, thus showing their respect for Paul (v. 16). In any event, said the apostle, the important thing was that Christ was preached, whatever the motives (v. 18), and that made him joyful.

1:15 It is true that some preach Christ

Besides imprisonment Paul experienced another troublesome situation. The words "it is true that" (in Greek, the single word μέν, *men*, "indeed") may imply that the Philippians had heard of it. The preaching of Christ, referred to in verse 14, was being done appropriately by some, but by others with tainted motivations. It has been argued that the two groups spoken of in these verses were sub-groups of the brothers who spoke courageously, to whom verse 14 referred. Careful examination of the text, however, would indicate that those whom Paul complimented in verse 14 would not be spoken of disparagingly here. Therefore we assume that he spoke of another situation in this verse.

out of envy and rivalry, but others out of goodwill.
Paul's concern here was motives, not message. There is no suggestion that what was proclaimed was heretical. Conjectures about those who preached out of envy and rivalry have been varied. Some have said their intent was to hasten Paul's punishment in the belief that such tribulation would hasten the return of the Lord. Others have argued that the preaching of Christ had been done against the Jews (see chapter 3) and the intent was to use the imprisonment to embarrass them, rather than to increase Paul's difficulties. Others have held that some believed Paul should accept martyrdom, and they were trying to increase the likelihood it would occur. Another view is that some believed Christianity would triumph immediately, and Paul's imprisonment seemed a denial of that. Therefore they opposed him because his situation conflicted with their theology. We believe the circumstance was a matter of rivalry. Certain church members aspired to positions of leadership and to the accolades and acceptance that came with that. Consequently they did what they could to increase Paul's difficulties, on the premise that the more he was subdued, the more their cause would be amplified. Thus they preached the correct message, but their intent was not so much to lead men to Christ as to enhance their own prestige as "leading figures" in the church. Though no view may answer all the questions, a lust for importance can explain the words "envy," "rivalry" (v. 15), "selfish ambition" and "not sincerely" (v. 17).

The words "envy" (φθόνος, *phthonos*) and "rivalry" (ἔρις, *eris*) often occur together in Paul, and only he uses the latter word in the New Testament. "Good will" could indicate good will toward Paul, or toward God. In the latter case the idea would be that those who preached Christ in the appropriate way were grateful for God's good will toward Paul.

1:16 The latter do so in love,

As with the interpretation of good will (v. 15), so "love" in this verse can be understood as love for Paul, or for God, or for the lost. But it may be stretching the text too far to attempt to make such distinctions here.

knowing that I am put here for the defense of the gospel.

The last of this verse relates to the ideas of verse 14. The words "put here" often conveyed the sense of divine appointment. Was Paul saying that he was put on earth to preach the gospel, or, more likely, that he was put in prison for the defense of the gospel? Was he referring to God's mandate to preach as the cause of his imprisonment, or to the imprisonment as an opportunity given by God? In the latter case even the harmful designs of men would work to the glory of God. Since God cannot be thwarted by human intent, what of those in verse 17 who were attempting to thwart God's will by corrupt motivations? "Defense" is the Greek word ἀπολογία (*apologia*) from which we get our word "apology." It referred to Paul's coming trial.

1:17 The former preach Christ out of selfish ambition, not sincerely,

In this carefully structured paragraph Paul turned to the second of the groups mentioned two verses earlier. Unfortunately there were those who put their own egos and self-enhancement above God himself and above the salvation of mankind. As Melick suggests, all of the groups in the church knew Paul, but not all welcomed him.[1] We might also infer

---

[1]Richard Melick, *Philippians, Colossians, Philemon* (Nashville: Broadman, 1991), p. 77.

from Paul's knowledge of the situation that their motives and opposition were not concealed.

supposing that they can stir up trouble for me while I am in chains.

The word "trouble" (θλῖψις, *thlipsis*) indicates inner distress or pain. We do not know the exact significance of this. Perhaps it implied inward annoyance or implied Paul's frustration because his imprisonment limited him. Perhaps some thought his imprisonment could be made more severe, or that his influence on the outside, especially in the church, could be diminished.

1:18 But what does it matter? The important thing is that in every way, whether from false motives or true, Christ is preached.

Paul's response to all this was remarkable. When one compares the severity of his language in other texts, as in Gal 1:8-9, these words appear most charitable. Perhaps Paul had mellowed as he aged. In this case, however, it was not the message that was threatened, as in Galatians. Rather it was a question of motivation. What people heard was what people ought to hear, regardless of the reasons it was proclaimed. Certainly Paul would argue the character of ministers was important, but he also recognized that the nature and power of the message would do their work regardless of the character of the minister. Truth is truth, despite the mind or mouth from which it comes. Paul here rose above any personal irritation or hostility to achieve a more noble perspective. The preaching of Christ, even from wrong motives, was for him a cause of joy.

And because of this I rejoice.

Here the verb for "rejoice" (χαίρω, *chairō*) is used, as elsewhere in 1:25; 2:2,17,18,28,29; 3:1; 4:1,4,10 (cf. notes at 1:4). Someone has said this was an extraordinary statement from an extraordinary man.

It is possible there was more to this issue than is indicated here. Paul's focus, however, was on the preaching of Christ, and he simply had no interest in developing more fully the exact circumstance that prevailed.

Why had he told this to the Philippians? Certainly to inform them about his situation. But he may also have recognized that problems of self-aggrandizement characterized the church in many places. He may have felt so strongly that he was giving the Philippians an indirect warning, even if he saw no immediate problem among them. Has the church ever been free from the problems caused by human ego wishing to transcend God's glory? Paul's veiled warning is appropriate in every age.

C. TO LIVE IS CHRIST, TO DIE IS GAIN (1:18b-26)

Yes, and I will continue to rejoice, [19]for I know that through your prayers and the help given by the Spirit of Jesus Christ, what has happened to me will turn out for my deliverance.[a] [20]I eagerly expect and hope that I will in no way be ashamed, but will have sufficient courage so that now as always Christ will be exalted in my body, whether by life or by death. [21]For to me, to live is Christ and to die is gain. [22]If I am to go on living in the body, this will mean fruitful labor for me. Yet what shall I choose? I do not know! [23]I am torn between the two: I desire to depart and be with Christ, which is better by far; [24]but it is more necessary for you that I remain in the body. [25]Convinced of this, I know that I will remain, and I will continue with all of you for your progress and joy in the faith, [26]so that through my being with you again your joy in Christ Jesus will overflow on account of me.

[a]*19* Or *salvation*

Paul continued to rejoice (v. 18) because he knew that the prayers of the Philippians and the help of the Spirit would produce his deliverance (v. 19). He anticipated that he would not be ashamed, but would have courage that Christ would continue to be exalted in his life, whether he lived or died (v. 20). For him to live was Christ; to die was gain (v. 21). If he continued to live he would labor for the Lord, but he did not know which option to choose (v. 22). In his dilemma he wished to depart and be with Christ, which was better (v. 23), but felt a call to remain in the body for the sake of his brothers (v. 24). Thus convinced, he said he would remain and continue with the Christians for their progress and joy in the faith (v. 25) so that by his reunion with them they would all rejoice in Christ Jesus.

Several interpretive problems surface in this paragraph. First, what is meant by "deliverance" (σωτηρία, *sōtēria*) in verse 20? Does it deal with release from prison, or was there a more spiritual significance? Secondly, what did Paul anticipate: release from prison, or the possibility that he would suffer capital punishment? Further, was prison really Paul's main concern? Would it not more likely have been the proclamation of Christ?

Paul's theme has been the preaching of Christ. In verse 14 he had expressed gratification that the brothers had preached courageously and fearlessly, as Paul's situation in prison had encouraged them. In verse 18 he had rejoiced that Christ was preached even though some did so from false motives. Now he elaborates the idea of being in chains for Christ (v. 13), but rejoices that not even his present experience could diminish his commitment to and service for Jesus Christ.

1:18b Yes, and I will continue to rejoice,

As in the end of the previous paragraph Paul had rejoiced because Christ was preached, now he continued to rejoice, because of his own experience of having been blessed by prayer and by the help of God's Spirit. Again we are impressed at Paul's joy in distressing circumstances.

1:19 for I know that through your prayers and the help

given by the Spirit of Jesus Christ, what has happened to me will turn out for my deliverance.

Paul knew that he would be delivered, and he knew that the prayers of the Philippians and the help of the Spirit of Christ had been crucial. For what had the Philippians prayed? Our understanding of the content of their prayers will depend on the understanding of the term "deliverance." In addition to prayer Paul spoke of the help of the Spirit. These two are often closely linked in Scripture (Luke 11:13; Acts 4:30f.). We are convinced that the Spirit operates in response to human prayer. The Philippians prayed, and God responded through his Spirit. If the distinction is even significant, we would argue that Paul spoke both of the possession of the Spirit, and of the help given by the Spirit. We recall the promises of Jesus in Mark 13:11; Matthew 10:20; and Luke 12:12. Paul here recognized a higher force than that possessed by his jailers and by the powers that put him in prison. When Paul spoke of "what has happened" he may have referred to the basic fact of his imprisonment, but it is quite likely he was also referring to those matters described in verses 12-18 (being in chains for Christ, the courage of the brothers, and the motives by which Christ was preached.)

We come now to the crux of this passage, the word "deliverance." The NIV footnote suggests the alternate reading "salvation." The Greek word σωτηρία (sōtēria), is often translated "salvation" in the New Testament. At least four suggestions have been given for the meaning of this word. (1) Release from imprisonment. (2) Inner spiritual strength for Paul in his circumstances. (3) A vindication of the message Paul preached. (4) Eternal salvation. Most commentators opt for (1) or (4). If Paul were speaking about release from prison, how could he have such conviction that it would occur? Though in verses 25f he seems to express a like confidence, it is difficult to know, given the overall tenor of his words, whether he would have absolute assurance. Furthermore, in 2:17 he seems again to contemplate the possibility of his death. Did he anticipate release, or did he think that if he were released it was clear he would continue to serve Christ, and thereby benefit the Philippians? On the other hand, if "deliverance" referred to eternal salvation, the idea may be that their prayers gave him the ability to endure, so that he would not be ashamed or in some way deny Christ (cf. v. 20) and thus would be assured of vindication at judgment. It may not be necessary to accept any of these options. Verse 20 may be a modification of the word "deliverance" and Paul may have been saying that he was in a "no lose" situation. It seems to us that the issue of imprisonment was of less importance to Paul than the issue of living for Christ and serving him. Prison was discussed as it impinged on the matter of Christian service.

It should be noted that the expression "turn out for my deliverance" is an exact quotation of the Septuagint of Job 13:16. In that context Job, though fearful, said he would still approach God, because he was convinced of his own right-eousness. This could be applied to Paul's coming trial, but it could also be applied to his standing before God. It should be noted that in verse 20 Paul spoke of shame and courage, picking up the themes from Job. This parallel may be the reason why the Job passage was employed here.

1:20 I eagerly expect and hope that I will in no way be ashamed, but will have sufficient courage so that now as always Christ will be exalted in my body, whether by life or by death.

Certainly the rigors of imprisonment and the shame of being jailed had the possibility of destroying faith. Even Paul recognized the threat. As in verse 14 he expressed thanks for the courage of the brothers in the Lord, so now he discussed the same with regard to himself. "Eagerly expect" (one word, ἀποκαραδοκία, *apokaradokia*, in Greek) is a strong term indicating one who strains forward with total energy and who has turned aside from all other interests. It was a strong way to express confidence in the help of God. Paul expressed himself first negatively (he would not be ashamed), and then in two positive ways (first, courage, and then the exaltation of Christ in his body.) "Ashamed" (αἰσχύνομαι, *aischynomai*) has an interesting heritage. In the Old Testament and the Dead Sea Scrolls it referred to the humble pious persons who trusted that God would not allow them to be shamed. Though some see the term as referring to shame at judgment, we are convinced it means shame before men, which shame might have kept Paul from exalting Christ in his body. He was not ashamed of being in prison, nor of being imprisoned for Christ. "Courage" could refer to courage in trial, but it more likely had a broader meaning, as indicated by the words "whether by life or by death." The expression "life or death" was Paul's way of indicating his absolute dedication to Christ. Verse 21 will explain the expression more fully.

The term "death" (θάνατος, *thanatos*) may not mean that Paul here anticipated the end of his life, but might simply be a way of showing that he would glorify Christ in any circumstance.

1:21 For to me, to live is Christ and to die is gain.

This verse explains what Paul meant in verse 20. At the same time it gives one of the great statements of personal conviction and one of the outstanding devotional texts of the entire New Testament. The reader is always challenged to ask if he or she could make this their own personal statement. Paul would speak particularly of his own perspective in verses 21-24. There is a contrast drawn all the way through. Life is Christ, life is worthwhile work, life benefits others; death on the other hand is gain, death is to be with Christ. Paul could in no way lose or be defeated. His whole life was centered in Christ. Since he had been discussing preaching and since we know this was the driving force of his life, we presume here that he had preaching (evangelistic and hortatory) in mind. Certainly, however, we cannot limit the term to that. "Fruitful labor" (v. 22) implies more than interior spiritual development; rather it indicates activity on behalf of others.

Verse 23 will show why dying in Christ was gain. Some suggest, in addition, that if one were to die a martyr's death, that

death would glorify Christ as well. Paul's gain was to be with
Christ. It is doubtful that Paul was expressing a sense of relief
that death would deliver him from earthly troubles. In fact, in
Romans 5:3-5 Paul expressed some sense of joy even in suffering. Hawthorne has paraphrased this magnificent statement
by saying that Paul could see no reason for being, except to
be for Christ.[2]

**1:22 If I am to go on living in the body, this will mean fruit-
ful labor for me. Yet what shall I choose? I do not know!**

Paul continued his meditation, in a verse which is somewhat
obscure in the Greek. Some have suggested that the disjointed
style may be because Paul wrote with intense emotion.
However he was certainly emotional in other parts of this letter
in which the style is not as chaotic as here. As the NIV reads
the idea is that if Paul were to continue living he could continue reaping the fruit of his toil. This seems to us the preferable
translation. Others have suggested that Paul was saying that if
living meant reaping fruits of his past toil, he wasn't sure which
to prefer. Still others argue that Paul was saying that if living
meant he would be able in the future to reap the fruit of his
toil, he did not know which to prefer. Though there are transla-
tional problems we believe the option we have chosen fits best
with Paul's words in verses 24 and 25. When Paul said "I do not
know" he may be indicating that he had received no revelation
about the issue of life or death. The Greek term rendered
"know" (γνωρίζω, *gnōrizō*) was always used by Paul to indicate
"making known" or revealing something. Thus he is not expressing indecision about his choice. Hawthorne suggests "I
cannot tell" better reflects the Greek.[3] He leaves the matter in
God's hands. If so, this would indicate that verse 20 was not
referring to his release from prison. Paul was choosing this way
to indicate that service for Christ would be a blessing and a
profit regardless of his destiny.

---

[2]Hawthorne, *Philippians*, p. 45.
[3]Ibid., p. 47.

1:23 I am torn between the two:

When Paul said "I am torn between the two" he used a word (συνέχομαι, *synechomai*) which indicated pressure from two equally strong desires, bearing upon him from either side. Whichever way Paul went the opposite urging would bear upon him as strongly as the decision he chose. It was not a matter of sacrificing a greater desire for a lesser.

Notice the parallel Paul makes in this and the following verses. To depart and be with Christ was better for him; to remain in the body was more urgent for them. Paul chose to remain, and thus set an example of service and humility. This is an important point, because in subsequent verses, beginning with verse 27, Paul's exhortation would call the Philippians to service and humility. He would bring before them the example of Christ (2:5-11), and later in chapter two the examples of Timothy and Epaphroditus (vv. 19ff). But first he offered his own example. Thus with his example, the reference to Christ, and the references to Timothy and Epaphroditus he made a fourfold illustration of his point. All, however, centered in the example of Christ.

I desire to depart

The term for "depart" (ἀναλύω, *analuō*) is used in other contexts of the military breaking camp, or of a ship being released from its moorings. So, were Paul to be released, what of those left behind? It was this meditation that occupied him in verse 24.

and be with Christ, which is better by far;

He spoke of being "with Christ." If one were to take all the Pauline texts that deal with the destiny of the righteous after death, it would still not be clear how all the details fit together (cf. 1 Cor 15:35-55; 1 Thess 4:13-5:10). Here in Philippians 3:20-21 Paul seems to indicate a period of awaiting the return of the Lord, at which time the righteous would be transformed into his image. In the present text, however, he seems to indicate he would be with Christ at death. Speculations on this issue do not reveal a totally satisfactory picture. Paul, however, as was the case with Jesus, was no doubt convinced that being prepared for death was more important than being able to sketch the after-death landscape. What mattered was to be with Christ. God would deal with matters in an appropriate way, and there was no need for humans to be anxious about exactly how this would happen. Thus Paul was not interested here in speculation about the afterlife.

1:24 but it is more necessary for you that I remain in the body.

Paul now turns from what was better to what was more necessary. His concern for the good of others underlay what he would say in 2:4, when he would call for Christians to be concerned for the interests of others. Some have suggested he felt it was more necessary for him to remain in the body because he was still alive, and interpreted that as an indication that God had more for him to do.

1:25 Convinced of this, I know that I will remain, and I will continue with all of you for your progress and joy in the faith,

This verse is puzzling, for at first glance it seems to express a conviction of release, which we have already seen was questionable. It would make more sense to understand Paul as saying that he was convinced of the necessity of ministry. Thus if he remained he would work for the enhancement of the faith of the Philippians and of others. Thus Paul's confidence was not in his release, but in what he would do if he were released. He knew in any event, as verse 19 has indicated, that he would be delivered, whether he lived or died. Perhaps Paul was not primarily concerned here with the issues of life or death, but rather was concerned with the issue of service, and was using his own case to make that point to his readers. This idea of progress in faith picks up the language of verse 6, where he expressed confidence that God would continue to do a good work in the Philippians. It also picks up the idea of verse 12 where reference was made to advancing the gospel.

Note also the word "joy" (χαρά, *chara*). This paragraph had begun and is ending with this note. However, the word in verse 26 is a different Greek term.

1:26 so that through my being with you again

The reference to being with the Philippians again is subjected to the same variety of translations as the term "deliverance" earlier. The most logical interpretation is that he hoped to be released from prison and to rejoin them in Philippi. Some, however, would interpret it of the ultimate union of Christians at the second coming of the Lord. We prefer the first option.

your joy in Christ Jesus will overflow on account of me.

Paul spoke of "overflowing joy." The word καύχημα (*kauchēma*) translated "joy" here in the NIV is rendered in some translations as "boasting" and in others as "glory." It may have been their joy in Christ because of what he had done through Paul and through them. Or it may have been their joy in the fact that Paul had been released. It has been argued that Paul was concerned that were he released they should not rejoice in him, but rather rejoice in what Christ had done.

III. ONENESS THROUGH SERVICE (1:27–2:18)

A. EXHORTATION TO A UNIFIED STAND (1:27-30)

[27]Whatever happens, conduct yourselves in a manner worthy of the gospel of Christ. Then, whether I come and see you or only hear about you in my absence, I will know that you stand firm in one spirit, contending as one man for the faith of the gospel [28]without being frightened in any way by those who oppose you. This is a sign to them that they will be destroyed, but that you will be saved — and that by God. [29]For it has been granted to you on behalf of Christ not only to believe on him, but also to suffer for him, [30]since

you are going through the same struggle you saw I had, and now hear that I still have.

To this point Paul has been giving biographical information. He will do this subsequently in 2:19–3:14 and 4:10-20. In verse 27 he begins his first section of exhortation, which will continue through 2:18.

The Philippians are called upon to conduct themselves in a manner worthy of the gospel of Christ, whether Paul was present or absent. This involved standing firm in one spirit and in a unified way contending for the gospel (v. 27). This contending was to be without fear from opponents. This would be a sign that the opponents would be destroyed, but that the Christians would be saved by God (v. 28). Verses 29 and 30 speak of belief and of suffering as gifts of Christ, with which both Paul and the Philippians could identify because of their experiences.

1:27 Whatever happens, conduct yourselves in a manner worthy of the gospel of Christ.
The first sentence stands as a heading for this entire section of exhortation. The exhortation is defined specifically in the next sentence as standing firm in unity and in unity contending for the gospel. In addition to the exhortation to unity, which implies a problem with disunity, Paul also speaks in the next verse of the need to overcome fear. Paul, in verse 6, had already expressed confidence in the growth that God would produce in the Philippians and had prayed for them to have a discerning love in verse 11. He had referred to their prayers for him in verse 19 and in verse 25 he spoke again of their progress in the faith. Now, however, he begins to specifically address problems in the church, and these themes, especially the theme of unity, will be sounded again and again through the letter.

"Whatever happens" translates a Greek word, μόνος (*monos*), which conveys the idea of the one essential thing. It focuses attention on the next few words of Paul. The call to worthy conduct was one issued to a community, so that Paul was dealing with more than personal piety. Though the issue has been debated, it has been suggested that Paul's words had as their background the pride that citizens of Philippi would take in their citizenship. Thus he would have said they should be concerned to let their "citizenship" as Christians be appropriate, as people in Philippi were concerned about their Roman citizenship.

Then, whether I come and see you or only hear about you in my absence, I will know that you stand firm in one spirit, contending as one man for the faith of the gospel

Paul called upon them to be faithful, whether he was present or absent. Their obedience was not because of him, but rather because of their relation to the Lord. One wonders if there is any subtle indication of what Paul might do were he to come and find the problems in the church still unresolved. The call to stand firm makes specific what "worthy conduct" has said in a more general way. The call would be repeated in 4:1. It may be a military usage, implying the idea of a soldier standing firm at his post. This firmness of spirit was expressed outwardly in their contending for the gospel. The word συναθλέω (*synathleō*), translated "contending," is composed of the root for our word "athlete" prefixed by the preposition "with." They were to be athletes with each other as one man.

Notice the twofold use of "one" in this verse. It was a basic premise of Paul's exhortations.

1:28 without being frightened in any way by those who oppose you.

In addition to a unified firmness, which led to struggle for the gospel, the Philippians were not to be frightened in the face of opposition. This exhortation implied that they may have been frightened, or even that their fear had in some way created compromise. The nature of the opponents is problematic. Some would suggest the false teachers of chapter 3, but the language indicating fear does not seem to fit the problem described there. Further, in verse 30 Paul seems to imply persecution from outside, likely from pagan forces. For that reason we prefer to think that they were outsiders who in some way were responsible for persecuting the church. The rest of Philippians, however, is silent about such a group.

This is a sign to them that they will be destroyed, but that you will be saved —

There has been considerable discussion about the "sign" in the last sentence. What was it? Was it the faith, or the steadfastness of the Christians, or their suffering, or was the opposition itself a sign of destruction? Perhaps the meaning of the sentence would not change regardless of which of these alternatives we choose. The second question is whether the sign would be recognized by the opponents. Some indicate that they would recognize from the events themselves that they would be destroyed, but this seems a strange meaning unless we presume that God would force such a recognition upon them. Perhaps it is better to argue that whether the opponents recognized the sign or not, the gospel, if true, indicates that enemies of the faith would be destroyed and that the Christians would be saved. The expression is intended to encourage the Christians and assure them of God's working both to save and to condemn. This interpretation, however, is tentative. We must recognize that the text is difficult, and various conjectures and interpretations have been offered to explain words that do seem to be somewhat strange.

and that by God.

We would argue that "and that by God" indicates that the process of judgment that resulted in salvation or destruction was God's business.

1:29 For it has been granted to you on behalf of Christ not only to believe on him, but also to suffer for him,

Paul's statement about belief being granted is an unusual one, since the word for "granted" (χαρίζομαι, *charizomai*) comes from the same root as the word "grace" (χάρις, *charis*) in verses

2 and 7. It is as if Paul were saying they were graced, not only to have faith, but also to suffer. Perhaps they had not thought of suffering as a grace, but rather as a disgrace. Thus Paul issues a call to go beyond resignation to suffering, to a realization that there were privileges that could come through suffering. A certain identification with Christ, which was the center of their lives, was offered in this way (cf. Matt 5:10-12; Acts 5:41; 14:22; Rom 5:1-5; 1 Thess 3:3; 2 Tim 3:12; and 1 Pet 4:13). Paul would continue the theme of suffering for Christ in 3:7-10. Paul's oft repeated note of joy as he writes from prison is a demonstration of the grace that was given him even in suffering.

1:30 since you are going through the same struggle you saw I had, and now hear that I still have.

Here Paul identifies himself with the Philippians in struggle, implying they could rejoice as he rejoiced. "Struggle" here comes from the same root (ἀγών, *agōn*) as our word "agony." The struggle that Paul experienced was the same conflict that the Philippians experienced. There were not many conflicts but one basic conflict. Paul had gone through difficulty in Philippi, as indicated in Acts 16:19-40 and 2 Corinthians 11:25. This may have been the circumstance to which he referred when he said "you saw I had." But it was not over for Paul, for they heard that he still had struggles. Paul's dealing with the experience could encourage them to have a like endurance and faithfulness.

His suffering led to the advancement of the gospel, according to verses 12 and 13 of this chapter. Thus it was not a defeat, but rather a victory.

PHILIPPIANS 2

B. ATTITUDES PRODUCING UNITY (2:1-4)

¹**If you have any encouragement from being united with Christ, if any comfort from his love, if any fellowship with the Spirit, if any tenderness and compassion, ²then make my joy complete by being like-minded, having the same love, being one in spirit and purpose. ³Do nothing out of selfish ambition or vain conceit, but in humility consider others better than yourselves. ⁴Each of you should look not only to your own interests, but also to the interests of others.**

In verse 1, Paul gives four motivations, followed in verse 2 by the desired result — unity. Verse 3 prohibits acting from selfish ambition or vain conceit, but rather commands humility in placing others above self. The fourth verse counsels concern for the interests of others, in addition to concern for one's own interests.

The exhortations begun in 1:27 continue here. There unity was discussed in relation to facing external difficulties. Here the call is to internal unity within the church. The reader is still not aware of the exact contours of the Philippians' disunity, but we may suppose the addressees had no doubt as to Paul's meaning. A specific case of two women will surface in 4:2, but whether the problem had further dimensions is unknown. It is possible Paul may have counseled these Christians so they would avoid problems he had seen arise in other churches, but which may have been only beginning in Philippi.

2:1 If you have any encouragement from being united with Christ, if any comfort from his love, if any fellowship with the Spirit, if any tenderness and compassion,

A fourfold motivation in verse 1 is balanced by a fourfold result (though some say threefold) in verse 2. The fourfold "if" (εἰ, *ei*) is somewhat ironic. It was not meant to express doubt. Rather the implication was that they possessed the highest sort of motivation. To "if," the appropriate response would be a resounding, "Of course there are such motivations!"

Following Paul's usual procedure, exhortation is preceded by motivation (cf. the schemes of Eph, Col). Following Christ was a relationship in which divine realities existed, not just a rule-keeping religion. The Philippians, examining their own experience, could see the reality of what Paul was saying. Thus they should act in a way which was harmonious with what God had done for them. Paul's words put the matter of their behavior in as serious a light as they could imagine.

The words translated "encouragement" and "comfort" in the NIV carry the ideas of consolation or strengthening. On this reading the idea was that God would supply the strength necessary to acquire the characteristics listed in verse 2. It is also possible to understand both terms as being exhortations, thus implying the idea of command. Consequently, there could be no greater authority than the one calling them to unity. We prefer the first alternative, however.

There is no agreement about a theological progression in the sections of this verse. It is difficult to distinguish shades of difference in the meanings of the words translated "encouragement" (παράκλησις, *paraklēsis*) and "comfort" (παραμύθιον, *paramythion*).

"United with Christ" is literally "in Christ." But the idea was that people in union with the Lord must surely be united with each other. For this not to be the case would be monstrous.

"The Spirit" (πνεῦμα, *pneuma*) is generally held to be the Holy Spirit. Since the references to Christ and the Spirit both refer to what God had done, we may assume that "love" ("his" is not in the Greek) refers to God's love, though some would see it as Paul's love for the Philippians.

"Fellowship in the Spirit" could mean the fellowship which the Spirit created, or could refer to the possession of the Spirit by all believers. Possession of the Spirit was used as an argument against salvation by the law in Galatians 3:2, and as a strong reason for unity in Ephesians 4:4. On this view, which we favor, disunity was seen as destroying the unity which God created by his indwelling presence. Certainly the Spirit would not fight itself!

"Tenderness" (σπλάγχνα, splanchna) and "compassion" (οἰκ–τίρμοι, oiktirmoi) are seen by some as two qualities, and by others as parallel statements of the same quality. Splanchna was rendered "affection" in 1:8. The terms could refer to the qualities in God which made salvation possible, or to the call for the saved to have the like qualities. In Christian terms, however, the Christian qualities are impossible without the divine qualities; and with the divine qualities, the Christian qualities become essential characteristics of redeemed persons.

2:2 then make my joy complete

The cluster of expressions used here leaves no doubt of Paul's desire for unity among the Philippians. In addition to the motivations of verse 1, the apostle also anticipated the completion of his joy by their obedience. Already, in 1:4, he had expressed joy because of them. Note also his references to rejoicing in 1:18 (twice) and see the discussion at 1:4.

by being like-minded, having the same love,

"Like-minded" and "purpose" are from the same Greek root (φρόν–, phron). It was translated "feel" in 1:7, and is found often in the rest of Philippians (see the notes at 1:7). The terms express intent and disposition. More than intellectual agreement, Paul called them to commit to one another, as they were committed to Christ. In verse 5 he will describe this "attitude" as the same as that which was found in Christ

Jesus. Certainly there would be disagreements in Philippi, as there will always be when humans interrelate. But their unity on the basis of their relation to Christ was to transcend any differences. Their love for each other was their response to Christ's love for them.

being one in spirit and purpose.

"One in spirit" translates a single Greek word (σύμψυχοι, *sympsychoi*). "Purpose," as indicated, shows the basic direction of their lives, individually and communally.

2:3 Do nothing out of selfish ambition or vain conceit,

The power of this exhortation is carried by two negative terms ("selfish ambition" [ἐριθεία, *eritheia*] and "vain conceit" [κενοδοξία, *kenodoxia*]) and one positive one ("humility" [ταπεινοφροσύνη, *tapeinophrosynē*]). *Eritheia* was employed previously in 1:17 of those who preached Christ from unworthy motives. His own experience gave Paul ample insight into the dangers of this attitude, and gave an added edge to his exhortation here. Cf. also condemnation of this sin in 2 Corinthians 12:20 (factions) and Galatians 2:20. *Kenodoxia* is found only here in the New Testament. Both "selfish ambition" and "vain conceit" are stock words found in ancient catalogues of vices. "Vain conceit" has the root idea of "empty opinion, error." Thus it could depict a person who, though conceited, had no reason for it.

but in humility consider others better than yourselves.

In Christ, however, conceit was never appropriate. Though *tapeinophrosynē* was an uncomplimentary term to the Greek mind, the attitude of Christ had sanctified it and made it one of the most significant of Christian virtues. Humility was not a sense of worthlessness, but rather was manifested in concern for others. The last part of the verse "consider . . . yourselves" defines the term. By adopting this perspective and by drawing from the reality of Christ's deeds, "selfish ambition" and "vain conceit" could be overcome.

2:4 Each of you should look not only to your own interests,

The thought of the last of verse 3 continues here. As the NIV reads, the text does not forbid a measure of self-interest. But it does call for a dedicated concern for others when seen in the light of verse 3. Cf. what Paul says of Timothy in 2:21. The Christ hymn which follows, beginning in verse 6, shows the extremity to which Christ went in his concern for others — for humanity.

but also to the interests of others.

An alternate rendering of this verse omits the word "only," which is not in the Greek, and "also" (καὶ, *kai*), which is not in some manuscripts. On this reading Paul did not give any legitimacy to one's own interests, but only to those of others. This interpretation argues, therefore, that Paul was calling for an observation and imitation of the good qualities of other Christians. They should not be so self-centered they failed to observe and be motivated by the virtues of others. In the general sense these things are true, but in view of what Paul will say in 2:5-11, it seems better to adopt the translation of the NIV, with the meaning discussed in the previous paragraph. O'Brien has shown that the idea of "only" can be assumed here on the basis of other Greek texts, and that there is adequate manuscript evidence to keep "also."[1]

C. THE EXAMPLE OF CHRIST (THE CHRIST HYMN) (2:5-11)

**[5]Your attitude should be the same as that of Christ Jesus:
[6]Who, being in very nature[a] God,**

did not consider equality with God something to be grasped,

[7]but made himself nothing, taking the very nature[b] of a servant,

being made in human likeness.

[8]And being found in appearance as a man,

---

[1]Peter O'Brien, *Philippians* (Grand Rapids: Eerdmans, 1991), pp. 184-185.

he humbled himself
and became obedient to death —
even death on a cross!
⁹Therefore God exalted him to the highest place
and gave him the name that is above every name,
¹⁰that at the name of Jesus every knee should bow,
in heaven and on earth and under the earth,
¹¹and every tongue confess that Jesus Christ is Lord,
to the glory of God the Father.

ᵃ6 Or *in the form of*   ᵇ7 Or *the form*

It is generally agreed that these verses are a Christian hymn, inserted into the text here as a powerful enforcement of the epistle's call to humility (and thus to unity). Though it is more evident in the Greek, the form of these words differs from the surrounding text. There are certain stylistic characteristics which are not typical of the rest of the letter. More importantly, there is a significant heightening of theology here. Several important terms in these verses are not found elsewhere in the letter.

This is a christological statement unparalleled in the New Testament. The breadth of concept has led to reams of discussion by writers who have probed the meaning of various terms in the text.[2] Nowhere else is the self-emptying of Christ described as it is here. Indeed, the theological profundity of the passage far outstripped the needs of Paul as he employed it. Thus it can be assumed that its full significance was in its original hymnic form, and Paul has employed it in a "reduced" usage. Were it composed by Paul only for this occasion, such exalted (and puzzling) concepts would not be necessary. Craddock well notes that the context shows Paul was not having a christological debate. He also observes that the hymn itself has no moral message (although it offers an

---

[2]For the fullest treatment, see Ralph Martin, *Carmen Christi* (Cambridge: University Press, 1967).

excellent platform from which to give moral exhortation). Since Paul was advocating morality (humility) these words, if composed just for this letter, would certainly have included such a thrust.[3]

We assume, then, that prior to the writing of Philippians these words stood in another context. Some have suggested they may have been a brief compend of Christian teaching, but the omission of something as basic as even a reference to the resurrection argues against that. Lohmeyer, who was the first scholar to demonstrate these words were a hymn, argued that the early church sang it at the Lord's Supper. Others have considered it a baptismal hymn. Whatever the case, we presume the effectiveness of its use in Philippians indicates it would be familiar to the readers, surely from church usage, and that it was considered to be true.

Where did the hymn originate? A variety of views have been offered. Some argue that it originated outside Christian sources, either from pagan, philosophical, or Jewish quarters. Then the original was "baptized" and made Christian. Others argue it originated entirely within Christian circles, and was ready to hand for use by Paul. Hawthorne, for example, believes the foot washing episode in John 13 formed the conceptual background.[4] He grants that linguistic similarities with John 13 are few, but contends there are numerous contacts in subject matter.

Others believe Paul himself was the author. Objectors to this view point out the absence of certain Pauline themes (e.g. the resurrection) but respondents contend that hymns were not meant to be complete theological statements. Paul's hymn to love in 1 Corinthians 13, if original with him, does demonstrate his talent as a hymn writer. Some advocating Pauline authorship say these words preceded Philippians, while others feel Paul composed the hymn just for this letter. In the latter

---

[3]Fred Craddock, *Philippians* (Atlanta: John Knox, 1985), pp. 42-43.
[4]Hawthorne, *Philippians*, pp. 78f.

case, however, it seems strange Paul would go so far beyond the purpose and needs of the epistle. It should be noted, though, that the hymn does connect smoothly with 2:1-4, and it also prepares for the thought of 3:20f.

If, as seems most likely, the hymn preexisted its use here, was there any modification of the original in order to make it fit the present context? Here again many suggestions have been made, dealing largely with the strophic arrangement of the text (two stanzas or three?; where are the divisions?). Special attention has been given to "even death on a cross" (v. 8), since it seems to violate the previous literary structure of the hymn. These analyses are complicated, however, by lack of knowledge of what the form of a hymn *should be*, as no set form of a hymn has been discovered to which comparison can be made. We are concerned to interpret the text as it stands, whatever may have been its prehistory.

Whatever the truth, once the hymn did not exist, and then it did. The realities described were made known to the church by what God did in Christ and through the inspiration of the Holy Spirit. The descriptive language used, which, as we shall see, poses many perplexing problems, may spring from the fact that such realities can only be expressed in ways that leave considerable latitude for the mystery of divine being and action.

There are certain pitfalls to avoid in interpreting these verses *in the context of Philippians*. One can easily become intrigued with exploring the meaning of the various statements about Christ ("very nature," "equality," "grasped," "made nothing," etc.) and thus forget the practical use to which Paul was putting these words. Another pitfall is the opposite. Preoccupation with the Pauline application can ignore the lofty theology of the text. A third pitfall is to expend all one's interpretive energy in trying to fathom the place of this hymn in early church life, considered as a text giving insight to early Christian worship. All of these inquiries have their place, but we must remember that we are primarily interpreting Philippians. We will be periodically presented with the problem of the original meaning of an expression in the hymn as compared to Paul's meaning.

Though some would analyze the text in terms of Christ's preexistence, his earthly life and his glorification, a simpler and more obvious division has verses 6-8 as one section, and verses 9-11 as a second.

2:5 Your attitude should be the same as that of Christ Jesus:

These words are not a part of the hymn, but introduce it and form a link with verses 1-4.

"Attitude" is from the same root (*phron*) as "minded" and "purpose" in verse 2 (cf. notes at 1:7). Any uncertainty about Paul's meaning there is now to be marvelously clarified. Further, "humility" of verse 3 is what verses 6-8 describe so powerfully.

The literal translation of these Greek words would be something like "think this among yourselves which also in Christ Jesus." Because this expression is somewhat vague, two distinct views of the verse have emerged. One contends that "in Christ Jesus" means "in union with Christ Jesus" or "in the church" or "as Christians." Paul reminded the Philippians of their conversion, and in his exhortation called them back to that commitment. Thus the focus was a call to reaffirmation of the new life. This view gives more emphasis to the meaning of the hymn as it existed outside Philippians.

A second interpretation, commonly known as the ethical view, considers Christ as a model to be followed. The NIV translation implies this meaning, but we must remind ourselves that any translation of the verse is somewhat interpretive. On this understanding Paul was not simply saying "remember and imitate" Christ, for in verse thirteen he said it was "God who works in you . . . ." Cf. other calls to imitate Christ in Romans 15:1-7; 1 Corinthians 11:1; 2 Corinthians 8:9; and 1 Thessalonians 1:6.

These two possibilities continue to be debated. The first has been more popular in recent years, though not universally accepted. The reader may well ask if, in the long run, there is that much difference between the new life in Christ Jesus and a personal imitation of Christ. The question is well asked, considering the ultimate nature of Paul's appeal.

The form of "your" (ἐν ὑμῖν, *en hymin*, "in/among you") indicates Paul was thinking of the attitude of the Philippians to one another. The verb φρονέω (*phroneō*, "think" or "be intent upon") has been rendered by some passively ("let this mind be" – KJV; compare the NIV), and by many more recent translations actively ("think this" [way]). Paul described the actions of humility on Jesus' part, but he was even more concerned with the inner thoughts that produced such actions. Of course no one can truly "get inside the mind" of Jesus, but certain things can be safely assumed, as in the present verses.

2:6 Who, being in very nature God,

On the christological level, the interpretive dilemmas here concern the meaning of "nature" and the meanings of "equality" and "grasped." The sort of subtle analysis demanded in interpreting these words is fascinating, but is probably also considerably more complicated than was Paul's hortatory intent in using them.

Though interpreters generally consider this a picture of the preexistent Jesus, some suggest the earthly Jesus may be in view here as well. "Being" is an indefinite term, so it cannot settle the time of which the text speaks. However the sense of emptying and humiliation seems more powerful if we assume Christ's preexistence is what is considered.

"Nature" translates the Greek μορφή (*morphē*). The term is found elsewhere in the New Testament only in 2:7 and in Mark 16:12 (the resurrected Jesus appeared in a different "form"). The scarcity of references means there is no other New Testament evidence on the basis of which to interpret the present text. Numerous meanings for the term have been offered and refuted. They include: (1) the essential nature of God; (2) the glory of God; (3) the image of God, as in Gen 1:27; (4) a mode of being for God; (5) and position or status vis-a-vis God. Without wading through all these conjectures, we believe Paul is saying, however cautiously, that Christ was

God! We should remember, too, the parallel with verse 7. Whatever the basic meaning of *morphē* in the one place, the same should be said of the other. Thus he was God (here) and he was a servant (v. 7).

did not consider equality with God something to be grasped,

Many interpretations (one author has surveyed over 20) have been offered of this text. We assume equality was already the possession of Christ Jesus, not something to which he aspired. "Grasp" (from ἁρπάζω, *harpazō*) means to snatch or seize, and in the passive sense indicates a prize; i.e., the thing seized. Christ did not use the equality to escape service and humiliation. It might be supposed that divinity would avoid the destiny described in the next two verses. But the idea seems to be the opposite. The servant God, because he was God and because his love and power made it possible, gave/emptied himself. His self-emptying was not a "contradiction" of God's nature, but a demonstration of it. This is surprising and wonderful. Hawthorne suggests the point could be made clearer if the first of the verse were translated "Precisely because he was in the form of God . . . ."[5]

In interpreting this verse we come into deep waters. If these suggestions are not correct, we think something more marvelous is. The more one meditates on the reality expressed by these words, the richer the divine care for man appears. Any reader sensing the power of this exhortation should surely be moved to humility and service.

2:7 but made himself nothing, taking the very nature of a servant, being made in human likeness.

The double level of interpretation certainly forces its attention on the reader here. At the christological level questions arise like "what did he give up when he 'made himself nothing'?"; "to what or whom did he make himself a servant?"; "what is the background of the word 'servant'?"; "is 'servant'

---

[5]Hawthorne, *Philippians*, p. 85.

the same as 'human likeness' or does it imply more?"; and "does 'likeness' imply full acceptance of and identification with humanity?" These issues lead one into the loftiest realms of human thought. Conjectured solutions must often say "about such mysteries we cannot be sure."

At the practical level, however, we must recall that Paul was making a point about human behavior. It was not his main purpose here to explore loftier issues of exact christo-logical definition. We cannot know the depth of insight of the hymn. But we do know that Philippians is a practical, not a speculative, letter.

We have noted that the self-emptying of Christ showed the love and condescension of the "servant God." It is clear from these words ("made himself") that Christ's action was volun-tary, not coerced. We assume this verse describes the incarna-tion itself, not Christ's actions once he became man. Those are described in verse eight.

The verb translated "made himself nothing" is ἐκένωσεν (ekenōsen). From it we derive the word "kenotic." The kenotic theory maintains that at the incarnation Christ gave up his omnipresence, omniscience, and omnipotence. He retained, however, qualities such as holiness, love, and righteousness. This view, though worthy, is probably asking more of this text than it says. But it does indicate how scholars have labored to understand what it was that Christ gave up when he "made himself nothing." Suggestions include divesting himself of his glory; or of his exercise of authority as God; or of his majesty; or of equality with God. Does it mean he gave up whatever kept him from being subject to the circumstances and vicissi-tudes of being human? Whatever the ultimate truth, Paul is more concerned with what God became, than with exactly what the specifics of that transition involved. His emptying is more fully defined in verse 8. As O'Brien says, he poured himself out totally for man's sake — whatever that meant![6] Again, we must marvel at the magnitude of the divine mercy!

---

[6]See the full discussion in O'Brien, *Philippians*, pp. 216-227.

How can God, who is everything, make himself nothing? If this consideration does not carry one into the regions of awe, what can?

"Nature" is the Greek μορφή (*morphē*), the term also used in verse 6 (see notes there). "Servant" is from the Greek δοῦλος (*doulos*), which means "slave" (see 1:1). This is the only place this term is used of Jesus in the New Testament. Other texts describing him as a servant use a different Greek word. One could see "slavery" as standing in opposition to deity, as if Christ went from one situation to its contradictory opposite. But we have argued that *doulos* defines an aspect of the divine nature, rather than being a contradiction of it (see John 13:3ff).

Two views are taken of the relation of "servant" to "human likeness." One holds them to be parallel. The other sees a progression from the first to the second. We hold to the first view. Servanthood, on this premise, was basic both to the nature of God, and to the human condition. The former was voluntary; the latter involuntary. God chose to serve. Man, though he may not recognize it, can be no other than a servant (including service to death, as the next verse shows). One might say, in paradoxical fashion, that "nothing is less like God than being a slave" and "nothing is more like God than being a slave."

What is the background from which the term "servant" is drawn? Some suggest Isaiah 53, but this view is open to objection for various reasons, including the fact that the word for "servant" there is παῖς (*pais*), not *doulos*. Another suggestion understands the text against the background of slavery in the society of Jesus' day.

"Being made" implies the conception and birth process. Birth and infancy are themselves risks, so they suggest again the helplessness to which Christ submitted himself. "Likeness" reiterates his complete identification with humanity.

The last line of verse 7, in the Greek, has been transferred to the first of verse 8 in the NIV.

2:8 And being found in appearance as a man, he humbled himself

The first part of the hymn concludes with this verse. To the power of the description "servant" in verse 7 is added the impact of "humbled" and "death on a cross." Paul's appeal to the Philippians was made with one powerful point after another.

Verse 7 described the fact of incarnation, and this verse depicts the nature of the incarnate life. "Now that the impossible has happened, and he is man, what will we see?" The answer is — humility! The very fact of practicing humility, so basic to the Christian lifestyle, and so contrary to the impulses of sinful and ego-centered man, is one men find exceedingly challenging and difficult. But Christ's way of living spoke volumes to the weakness of humans, and to the nature of the new life.

and became obedient to death —

To be human was to be subject to "death." But Paul added another marvel by reference to "death on a cross." From one perspective, how vast the contrast with "being in very nature God" of verse 6 and with "Lord" of verse 11. Jesus knew to be human was to die, but his obedient humanity led to the most disgraceful of deaths, as a despised criminal, intentionally humiliated, and subjected to intense sufferings.[7] Elsewhere Paul, stressing the shame of such a death, identified it with death on a tree, which was done to one accursed by God (Deut 21:23, quoted in Gal 3:13). Of course, Christ was not accursed by God, but it could seem that way because of how he died.

"Obedient" to whom? The text does not say, but we presume the meaning is obedience to God, which led to his terrible fate. Nor does the text indicate the benefit of Christ's deed on the cross for humanity. But the church would know it well, whether it were specifically stated or not.

---

[7]For an outstanding study of crucifixion in the ancient world see Martin Hengel, *Crucifixion* (Philadelphia: Fortress, 1977).

even death on a cross!

The role of the cross in this context prepares us for 3:18, where Paul speaks of "enemies of the cross of Christ." Whatever their exact identity, this text helps us see the enormity of their sin.

"Even death on a cross" seems to break the metric structure of the hymn. Was it original, or was it added here? Both views have been taken. Our task, however, is to understand the passage as it stands.

2:9 Therefore God exalted him to the highest place

The style of Greek changes in verses 9-11 from that of verses 6-8. One difference is the increased number of Old Testament constructions and allusions.

If the story had ended with "death on a cross" we would wonder at the intent of such voluntary divine humiliation. The dramatic reversal is saluted by the words "Therefore God." To this point Christ was the active party. Now he is passive, and the Father is active. The humiliated one becomes the exalted one. The slave becomes the Lord (vv. 9 and 11 — "name" and "Lord").

The contrast with verses 6-8 makes the reader gasp with amazement. The Greek makes the point as strong as possible with "exalted . . . highest place." The term ὑπερυψόω (hyperypsoō), used only here in the New Testament, goes beyond the usual word for exaltation. One author has suggested the meaning "super exalted," or "raised to the loftiest heights." The nature of the exaltation is described in the next two verses. The christological inquiries here have asked what aspect of Christ was exalted (contrast "made nothing" in v. 7) but Paul has not enlightened us on such issues.

The power of the exaltation is also conveyed by the contrast between the decisive totality of this description compared to the stages with which the humiliation was described.

and gave him the name that is above every name,

"Gave" is from a verb (χαρίζομαι, charizomai) which is cognate to the word for grace. The gracious divine bestowal was a name — and a reality. The name was not Jesus, for that would represent no advance on Christ's earthly status. Rather it was Lord (v. 11). He was named Lord because he was Lord.

So humiliation led in God's economy to exaltation. In the application Paul was not urging humility on the Philippians so they would be exalted. But exaltation would be the result. Jesus taught the same thing often during his ministry (cf. Luke 11:14; 14:11). Obedience to the admonition of 2:3 would lead to exaltation. Where would disobedience lead?

2:10 that at the name of Jesus every knee should bow,

At the pinnacle of all creation Jesus is to receive the homage of all that exists. Made triumphant by God, he receives universal worship. All will know of the great reversal. "The name of Jesus" means Jesus himself. Paul borrowed the language of Isaiah 45:23 in his references to every knee bowing and every tongue confessing. There are two views about this submission. One says that all creatures would gladly make such an acknowledgment in submission to him. The second says some would submit willingly, and others would acknowledge his Lordship without submission. Thus not all who bowed and confessed would be saved (cf. Rev 9:20f; 16:9,11). But no one would escape the mastery of his Lordship. Ultimately he would not be successfully resisted.

in heaven and on earth and under the earth,

There have been numerous attempts to define the nature of "heaven," "earth," and "under the earth." One writer said they were first invisible powers, then those alive now, and then the dead, respectively. Others have suggested angels, humans, and demons; and still others have suggested spirit powers thought to rule these three realms. Whether any of these views is elected, or some other, the point is that nothing is outside the sovereignty of Jesus. As a practical application Paul's readers should beware lest their divisiveness, selfish ambition and vain conceit (in attitude and deed) put them outside the realm of those freely acknowledging Jesus' Lordship.

2:11 and every tongue confess that Jesus Christ is Lord, to the glory of God the Father.

"Jesus is Lord" is held to be the earliest Christian confession (1 Cor 12:3; Rom 10:9; Col 2:6). Paul's words here reminded the church of the powerful realities lying behind that confession, and of the great obligation which making it imposed.

The climax is the "glory of God." This is the result of Christ's Lordship. It would also be the result of the acknowledgment of that Lordship in the "attitude" (v. 5) of the Philippians.

D. EXHORTATION TO OBEDIENCE (2:12-18)

1. Work Out Salvation (2:12-13)

[12]**Therefore, my dear friends, as you have always obeyed — not only in my presence, but now much more in my absence — continue to work out your salvation with fear and trembling, [13]for it is God who works in you to will and to act according to his good purpose.**

Here Paul makes further application to the Christ hymn, calling for an obedient response from the Philippians while he was absent just as they had obeyed when he was present. This continued working out of their salvation, to be done with fear and trembling, would be energized by God. Both their wills and actions would be so empowered according to the divine purpose.

2:12 Therefore, my dear friends,

Paul has described the behavioral needs of the church (1:27f; 2:2-4) and has offered the highest possible motivation. Now, building on this most impressive foundation he urges utmost seriousness and energy in their obedience. It must be kept in mind that these much-discussed verses are to be seen in context. They are part of the hortatory section that began in 1:27, and are the "invitation to action" following the hymn. The call was to humility and service, to unity and unselfishness (vv. 2-4). That was the apostle's focus, so that he is not here simply giving a general statement about the whole of the Christian life.

C.S. Lewis has observed how these verses tie human effort and divine empowering together in one text. The words warn against a view that says "salvation" comes solely by human effort. But they also warn against holding that divine grace is so overwhelming that humans need not exert the greatest effort in God's service. Glorious grace does not excuse from work. If work could earn salvation, the in-working of God would be unnecessary. If grace alone were sufficient, there would be no call for human effort. The mandate of verse 12 would be a frightening one (and has been for many) were it not for the promise of verse 13.

"Dear friends" indicates again the affection already expressed in 1:3-11. The reference to obedience is made more powerful by an understanding of Christ's obedience described in verse 8. How could a disciple of Christ, reminded of the wonder of the Lord's obedience, refuse to obey? And how could a disciple, commended for obedience, not feel the great compliment in view of Christ's obedience? The obedience, of course, would be to the injunctions stated in 1:27–2:5, but would also look forward to further exhortations within the letter.

as you have always obeyed — not only in my presence, but now much more in my absence —

When Paul spoke of his "presence" or "absence," he could have referred to the past or to the future, depending on how the Greek is understood. It is more important to know that they were responding to Christ, and this response did not depend on the presence or absence of any human being, including Paul.

continue to work out your salvation

"Salvation" has been the subject of considerable discussion. There are two views most often advocated. An older view holds that this was individual salvation. Since the work of J.H. Michael in 1924, however, others have maintained that the reference is sociological. Since the word σωτηρία (*sōtēria*) rendered "salvation" can also mean "wholeness" or "health," it is argued that the call was to seek the spiritual well being of the church. Hawthorne takes the latter position.[8] O'Brien, without denying the emphasis on the entire church, argues that individual salvation cannot be excluded.[9] It seems that Paul's call to unity in verses 2-4 must involve the whole community and its health. But how can one separate what the church is from the salvation of its members? Perhaps Melick best states the essence of the matter when he observes that Paul was telling them to act like Christians should![10] But the primary thrust of Paul, we maintain, was for the welfare of the Christian community.

with fear and trembling,

The word φόβος (*phobos*) translated "fear" is the root of our "phobia," and that rendered "trembling" (τρόμος, *tromos*) of our "trauma." The expression is frightening. But Paul was not speaking of apprehension about the final judgment. His intent was not to produce anxiety, but to promote seriousness and maximum dedication to the task. If we took "fear and trembling" to refer to apprehension of being eternally lost, this would seem to imply that the divine energizing of verse 13 would be of very little help. Hawthorne thinks the expression carries the sense of "obediently work."[11] How could one not practice such exertion, given the great reality described in verses 5-11?

---

[8]Hawthorne, *Philippians*, p. 98.
[9]O'Brien, *Philippians*, pp. 276-280.
[10]Melick, *Philippians*, p. 110.
[11]Hawthorne, *Philippians*, pp. 98f.

2:13 for it is God

To those who found the task of being Christian seemingly impossible, verse 13 offered glad news. Paul told his readers God had already been at work in them, and would continue to do so. Here the theme of growth, introduced in 1:6, resurfaces. "You can," because "God is." Thus, though maximum effort was demanded, doubt could be cast aside. Salvation does not depend solely on human effort. God calls men to his tasks, but then he works in them to realize the call. Also, they did not need Paul's presence to work, for they had God's presence.

who works in you to will and to act

"Work" in verse 13 (two times) is from the verb (ἐνεργέω, *energeō*) which yields our word "energy." Paul used the word eighteen times, of twenty uses in the New Testament. The divine energy provoked the human work. The process was one initiated by God. Human work was responsive to divine energy. God's activity affected both intent (will) and action.

according to his good purpose.

Since "his" is not in the Greek, some have suggested that "good purpose" refers to men, with a meaning such as "good will" or "good understanding." Thus, God works to produce good will in the church. This is linguistically possible, though we prefer to think that God's purpose to save man is the sense here.

2. Become Faultless Children (2:14-18)

[14]**Do everything without complaining or arguing,** [15]**so that you may become blameless and pure, children of God without fault in a crooked and depraved generation, in which you shine like stars in the universe** [16]**as you hold out[a] the word of life — in order that I may boast on the day of Christ that I did not run or labor for nothing.** [17]**But even if I am**

being poured out like a drink offering on the sacrifice and service coming from your faith, I am glad and rejoice with all of you. ¹⁸So you too should be glad and rejoice with me.

ª*16 Or hold on to*

2:14 Do everything without complaining or arguing,

One might suppose that conceit and disunity in the church would produce "complaining" (γογγυσμός, *gongysmos*) or "arguing" (διαλογισμός, *dialogismos*). So, as Paul had attacked the spirit of the problem, and had urged great earnestness in meeting it, he now specifies concrete action — which was to cover all circumstances ("everything"). Little (nothing?) is said elsewhere in the book about complaint or argument, but one wonders how this relates to the disaffection between Euodia and Syntyche in 4:2? Since the next verse reflects the language of Deuteronomy 32:5, some turn to the Pentateuch for enlightenment here, suggesting that Paul's readers would think of the complaints of the Israelites in the wilderness. Concrete details about the implications of the these words elude us, but we do presume the complaints and arguments were directed against each other, not against God, since it is unity within the church which Paul addresses throughout Philippians.

2:15 so that you may become blameless and pure, children of God

The words "blameless and pure" (ἄμεμπτος, *amemptos*, and ἀκέραιος, *akeraios*) echo Paul's prayer in 1:10. The terms doubtless had primary reference to the problems identified in 1:27–2:4, as well as to the previous verse. Paul had spoken previously of evangelism (1:12-14,15-18,27) and now he attacks the problems within the church that affected their outreach. He describes the world in two ways: as crooked and depraved; and as being in darkness. Children of God, if not blameless in the sense Paul described it, destroy the effectiveness of their main task — holding out the word of life (cf. John 17:20-23).

without fault in a crooked and depraved generation,

Why did Paul adopt the language of Deuteronomy 32:5 (*"crooked and depraved"*) to describe the "outside" world? It is possible that the language had no special implications from the Old Testament. Since Deuteronomy describes Israel's transgression, however, and since the language was here applied to the world, perhaps Paul wished to contrast a blameless church with a blameworthy Israel. Was there any implication that Israel's call to impact the world for God had failed? Further, the church now constituted the children of God, and was the true Israel. These suggestions about Israel, however, do not catch up a main theme in the book, though they do bear some relation to what Paul said in 3:2-11.

in which you shine like stars in the universe

"Shine" suggests Jesus' teaching in Matthew 5:14-16 about his followers being the "light of the world." The term for "stars" (φωστῆρες, *phōstēres*) refers to any light-giving body, and is rendered "lights" and "stars" in different translations. "Stars" is based on usage of the term in the LXX (cf. Dan 12:3). If translated "lights" reference could be to certain literary allusions describing great Israelites as light bearers. Whatever the meaning, the world is to be enlightened by the church, and the church cannot do that if riddled by dissension.

2:16 as you hold out the word of life —

What do God's blameless children do? They "hold out" (or "hold on to") the "word of life." If the translation "hold out" is to be preferred, then the idea of mission and outreach was prominent. But "hold on to" (NIV footnote) is also a possible translation. In that case steadfastness was emphasized (cf. 1:27f). A good case could be made for either meaning, since both steadfastness and evangelism can be documented within the letter. (Cf. the notes on v. 15, as well as 1:6; cf. "stand firm" in 1:27).

in order that I may boast on the day of Christ

Paul returns to a personal reference — the first since 1:6 —

in the last of this verse. "Boast" (καύχημα, *kauchēma*) was a term Paul used frequently (46 of 50 New Testament references are Pauline). The idea focused more on the reason for boasting than on a boast itself. He had previously given the main motivations that should move them, but he cannot avoid a personal note. He did not intend to gloat, but in his great love for the church he indicated how severe his disappointment should be if that love had been for naught. The "day of Christ" was previously mentioned in 1:6 and 10; and is referred to in different language in 3:20 (see also 2:10f). Paul set their faith in the context of final judgment, which reinforced the seriousness called for in verse 12.

that I did not run or labor for nothing.

Paul used two words for his ministry here. "Run" describes an athlete, an idea picked up in 3:12f. (cf. also Gal 2:2; 1 Cor 9:24-27). "Labor" (κοπιάω, *kopiaō*, "toil, work intensively") may modify "run," indicating the exertion involved, or it may be drawn from his work as a tentmaker. Both show how fully he had exerted himself on the behalf of the Philippians. He had nearly exhausted himself for their sake (cf. Col 1:29; 1 Tim 4:10).

2:17 But even if I am being poured out like a drink offering on the sacrifice and service coming from your faith, I am glad and rejoice with all of you.

If Paul's boast in verse 16 were misunderstood, here he "subordinates" his work to their "sacrifice and service." In so doing he gives another demonstration of his servant role, of which he had spoken in 1:25f, and which further carries the point made by the Christ hymn. His concern for their salvation was so intense that he found joy in whatever he had done to enhance it. He was the "man for them." This was the positive side, set in opposition to "for nothing" in verse 16.

The term for "poured out" (σπένδομαι, *spendomai*) is found as well in 2 Tim 4:6, where Paul contemplated his death. It is commonly believed the same meaning is found here. In verse

24 Paul speaks of hope for release, and in view of that we think the reference to death here describes the intensity of his dedication, not a possible death penalty from prison. He not only ran and labored, but he would die ("but even if"). Were he to be judicially executed that would be no benefit to the Philippians' "sacrifice and service," but his intense dedication would benefit them.

A drink offering would accompany a sacrifice, being poured atop it or at the foot of the altar (cf. 2 Kings 16:13; Jer 7:18; Hos 9:4). So whatever Paul endured for their sake completed their faith, as the libation completed the sacrifice. "Sacrifice and service" compliments the readers. Paul skillfully urged them to greater holiness by alternating compliment and command. "You are good, but you must be better." A libation was not significant if made alone, and Paul's work for them would lose its purpose if they did not continue to grow in obedience.

2:18 So you too should be glad and rejoice with me.

"Rejoice with" indicates either their joy in service, or joy over Paul's concern for them, or both. The first option seems most likely, since verse eighteen may be a call from Paul to rejoice in his work for them.

Some suggest the rejoicing of the Philippians in verse 17 was because of something different from that in which they were bidden to rejoice in verse 18. If so, we can only conjecture what it might have been. Perhaps, as suggested above, they and Paul found joy in their service, and now he called them to rejoice with him in his work as well. It is at points like this, however, that we should beware of being overly subtle in our interpretations.

IV. PAUL'S CO-WORKERS (2:19-30)

A. REGARDING TIMOTHY (2:19-24)

[19]I hope in the Lord Jesus to send Timothy to you soon, that I also may be cheered when I receive news about you.

²⁰I have no one else like him, who takes a genuine interest in your welfare. ²¹For everyone looks out for his own interests, not those of Jesus Christ. ²²But you know that Timothy has proved himself, because as a son with his father he has served with me in the work of the gospel. ²³I hope, therefore, to send him as soon as I see how things go with me. ²⁴And I am confident in the Lord that I myself will come soon.

Paul has referred to himself in verses 12-18. The next main personal section of this letter begins here and extends through 3:14. These biographical details, valuable to us for the detail about Paul, were not simply informational. Paul also used them for exhortation. In this passage about Timothy the basic information can be derived from verses 19, 23, and 24. Verses 20-22 compliment Timothy, but also further Paul's case for humility and service to others — a case already made in the Christ hymn (2:5-11) and by Paul's example (1:24-26; 2:17f). In the subsequent paragraph, dealing with Epaphroditus, Paul augments the basic information by noting Epaphroditus's humility and service (vv. 25,29f). Thus these two paragraphs, which some dismiss as insignificant personal data, are freighted with considerable hortatory significance.

This is the case, in fact, with all of the "personal" sections in Philippians, and may explain why Paul intersperses such material throughout the letter, rather than saving it to the end, as he sometimes does (cf. Romans, Colossians).

2:19 I hope in the Lord Jesus to send Timothy to you soon,

Paul hopes (ἐλπίζω, *elpizō*) to send Timothy (cf. 1:1), and in verse 24 he is confident (a different Greek word, πέποιθα, *pepoitha* [from πείθω, *peithō*, "persuade"]) he would come himself. Both statements place the events "in the Lord." The statement was not essential to the information, so why did Paul make it? Perhaps it was an affirmation of his faith that all plans of life are in God's hands, and thus he yielded to the divine purposes ("if the Lord wills"). He may have wished to avoid seeming to plan his plans apart from reliance on Christ. This would be especially true with the more tenuous possibility of his release implied by verse 24.

that I also may be cheered when I receive news about you.
Timothy was to be sent, apparently, to gather news about the Philippians and then return with it to Paul. We presume that in addition to personal information Paul would be greatly concerned that the problems of the church he addressed in the letter had been resolved. Very likely Timothy could be expected to contribute to such resolution, and perhaps to encourage the church in other ways. This seems implied by Paul's reference to Timothy's "genuine interest" in their welfare (v. 20). Further, Timothy could bring news to them of any further developments in Paul's case since they had received his letter. On other missions of Timothy for Paul see 1 Thessalonians 3:1-5; 1 Corinthians 4:17; 16:10; and cf. Acts 17:14f; 19:22.

"Cheered" is from a Greek word (εὐψυχέω, *eupsycheō*) that was often found on graves as a final wish for the dead. This is its only use in the New Testament.

2:20 I have no one else like him,
Timothy was with Paul when the church began in Philippi, and paid later visits to the city (Acts 19:21f; 20:3-6). His firsthand knowledge would at least partly account for his "genuine interest." This may be the significance of "no one else like him," i. e., no one else knows the church as he does. Yet we must keep in mind the words of verse 21.

who takes a genuine interest in your welfare.
"Take interest" (μεριμνάω, *merimnaō*) is the same term translated "be anxious" in 4:6. Obviously the meaning can be positive, as here, or negative, depending on context. The word is a strong one, implying that Timothy's concern bore heavily upon him.

2:21 For everyone looks out for his own interests, not those of Jesus Christ.

It is tempting to link these words with 2:3,4, which exhorted concern for the interests of others (cf. also the negative example of 1:15-17). If we make the connection it would seem Paul was criticizing those around him for failing to display the virtues he was urging. The problem was both in his locale and in Philippi.

Paul may have been scoring selfishness here, but a case can be made for a less harsh reading of the text. Some of those around Paul had been complimented for their evangelism (1:14). If Paul were in Rome, we know from Col 4:10,14 and Phlm 24 that he was accompanied by Aristarchus, Luke, Mark and others (unless some had departed by the time Philippians was written). Surely they would not be criticized for selfishness. On the basis of this evidence, it is held by some that of those "qualified" (knowing the church and having a personal concern) to go (a formidable mission) only Timothy was a possibility. Or that others had other work, not necessarily unworthy, that occupied them. We do not have sufficient information to determine the exact force of Paul's words. It may be some could not go for legitimate reasons, and others would not go because of a lack of real concern. We need not assume all of those who looked out for their own interests were of the same stripe. Yet in the final analysis "not those of Jesus Christ" seems decisively uncomplimentary, though the things of Jesus Christ would be primarily the needs of the church in Philippi, not the entire Christian life.

2:22 But you know that Timothy has proved himself,

If verse 21 were meant as a criticism, Paul did not elaborate, but returns to discuss Timothy. Their knowledge of him would be based, at least partly, on his earlier presence with them (cf. Acts 19:21f; 20:3-6). Why did Paul find it necessary to commend Timothy here? Was it just Christian appreciation for a faithful servant? Could the Philippians have previously seen Timothy as "second fiddle" to Paul, and the apostle wished to ensure they would see him as more than a subordinate? We prefer this latter alternative.

because as a son with his father he has served with me in the work of the gospel.

Paul uses two images to indicate Timothy's worth. First, "father" and "son" indicate the family and the closeness of those bonds (see 1 Cor 4:17; 1 Tim 1:2). Second, "served" (from δουλεύω, *douleuō*) is from the same root as the word for "slave," so Timothy's slavery to God showed his dedication (cf. 1:1). "With me" indicates Paul did not consider Timothy his slave, but God's slave.

2:23 I hope, therefore, to send him as soon as I see how things go with me.

These words modify "soon" of verse 19. But what is implied by "things go with me?" A natural assumption would be that Paul's trial was the issue, though he expresses confidence in verse 24. Others hold that Paul had other things in mind, perhaps personal needs or concerns for the church. We must recall that Paul at this time was probably in his seventh or eighth decade of life, with physical problems, and might need assistance a younger man could forego. Further, he needed someone to do what he in prison was not free to do. Apparently his concerns did not fall in the same category as those of the ones who looked out for their own interests, in verse 21.

Whatever his concern, Paul expected it to be dealt with before long, and Timothy to be sent on his way.

2:24 And I am confident in the Lord that I myself will come soon.

We have previously discussed (1:18b-26) the question of Paul's expectations of release. He has indicated his yearning for them in 1:8, and has referred to the possibility of coming in 1:26f and 2:12. This is his most optimistic statement yet in the letter and is the last statement on the subject. Whatever his case, he placed it in the Lord's hands. But we suspect he had some indication or strong suspicion of good news. But even if he should not come, Timothy would offer the church the ministry Paul wished them to have.

The word ταχέως (*tacheōs*) translated "soon" is literally "immediately," but the term is qualified by the implied situation after Timothy's trip to Philippi and return to Paul. The language may be used to emphasize that they need not wait long for Timothy to arrive.

B. REGARDING EPAPHRODITUS (2:25-30)

[25]But I think it is necessary to send back to you Epaphroditus, my brother, fellow worker and fellow soldier, who is also your messenger, whom you sent to take care of my needs. [26]For he longs for all of you and is distressed because you heard he was ill. [27]Indeed he was ill, and almost died. But God had mercy on him, and not on him only but also on me, to spare me sorrow upon sorrow. [28]Therefore I am all the more eager to send him, so that when you see him again you may be glad and I may have less anxiety. [29]Welcome him in the Lord with great joy, and honor men like him, [30]because he almost died for the work of Christ, risking his life to make up for the help you could not give me.

Now Epaphroditus is introduced. All we know of him is drawn from this paragraph and from 4:18. His name, a common one, is similar to Aphrodite, and means "lovely, charming, amicable." Some suggest, because of the similarity with Aphrodite, that he was a Gentile convert from a family which worshiped that goddess.

Paul continues his call to humility and service by presenting another example of such commitment. He compliments Epaphroditus five ways in verse 25, and then speaks further of his dedication in verses 29 and 30. A person who risked his life offered a strong contrast to those who were selfish and conceited, and who selfishly pursued their own interests, heedless of others (cf. 2:3f).

Though it is not stated specifically some scholars have assumed that it was the intent of Epaphroditus and of the Philippian church for him to be Paul's permanent helper. That plan was thwarted, however, by his sickness, and then by his subsequent and severe homesickness. We agree with this conjecture and with the view that Paul here was dealing with a delicate matter. Thus he gave generous commendation and comment on Epaphroditus's situation so that he would be received home with honor, rather than with criticism.

It is generally believed that Epaphroditus bore this letter to the Philippians. It is also possible, although less likely, that the letter was sent first by an unknown messenger, and that Epaphroditus came later. On the first view we see in verses 19-30 a threefold "mission" to Philippi. First Epaphroditus, then Timothy, and finally Paul. This speaks strongly of the apostle's great love and concern for this church.

2:25 But I think it is necessary to send back to you Epaphroditus,

"Send back" is in a form indicating complete action. Paul spoke from the viewpoint of the readers, to whom the return was an accomplished fact. "Back" is not in the Greek, so no assumption should be made from the English text that Paul had previously planned for Epaphroditus to return.

my brother, fellow worker and fellow soldier, who is also your messenger,

Epaphroditus is described in three ways that indicate his relation to Paul (cf. the words about Timothy in 1:22) and in two that indicate his relation to the church. "Fellow worker" (συνεργόν, *synergon*) is a Pauline expression (12 of 13 New Testament references). The obvious reference was to efforts with Paul in the latter's imprisonment. Perhaps Paul also had in mind previous joint efforts in Philippi itself. "Fellow soldier" (συστρατιώτης, *systratiōtēs*) may imply conflict and even suffering. "Messenger" (ἀπόστολος, *apostolos*) is literally "one sent" — the same word as "apostle." Compare a similar use of the term in 2 Corinthians 8:23. Though commonly used only of the twelve the term had broader senses and was therefore also used to describe others in the New Testament who were engaged in various missions. "Minister" translates a term the Jews applied to the priesthood. In that sense it may relate to the description of the gift Epaphroditus brought to Paul as a "sacrifice" (4:18).

whom you sent to take care of my needs.

The "needs" will be described more fully in 4:10-18, though if Epaphroditus was sent as a permanent minister/ assistant for Paul, they could be even broader than that text indicates.

2:26 For he longs for all of you and is distressed because you heard he was ill.

Philippians is full of expressions of strong affection of Christians for each other (cf. 1:7f,25f; 4:1) and the relation between Epaphroditus and the Philippian church was a case in point.

The illness of Epaphroditus would be the subject of the following verses. But the present verse could be understood as implying homesickness. If that were true, and since Paul knew of it, it might have been a pressure on him in addition to the anxiety (v. 28) he felt regarding Epaphroditus's physical health. "All of you," as with "all" in 1:1,4, may depict Epaphroditus as a man who was above the Philippian divisions. That may have been a further reason Paul sent him home — to help heal the breaches in the church.

Word of Epaphroditus's illness had reached Philippi, and then word of their concern had come back to Paul and Epaphroditus. This could imply an illness of considerable length, or that it had been some time since Epaphroditus had recovered. "Distressed" (ἀδημονέω, *adēmoneō*) is the same term used of Jesus' agony in Gethsemane. Epaphroditus was concerned about their concern. As for the illness itself, which was extremely serious (vv. 27,30), it may have been contracted on his journey to Paul, or during his stay with him. Some suggest he became sick on the journey, but pressed on heedless of his condition, which only worsened his state.

2:27 Indeed he was ill, and almost died.

Paul may have mentioned Epaphroditus's brush with death (literally "a near neighbor to death") because the Philippians were not aware of just how serious the case was. These words prepare for the praise of Epaphroditus in verse 30, in which a powerful exhortation to sacrificial service is implied.

But God had mercy on him, and not on him only but also on me, to spare me sorrow upon sorrow.

Epaphroditus's healing is attributed to God's mercy. The exact implications of this (miracle?) cannot be determined, but the text is another example of Paul's remarkable God- and Christ-centeredness (cf. 1:19,24,29). Had Epaphroditus died, which apparently had seemed quite possible, Paul's sorrow at his own incarceration would have borne the additional burden of grief at his friend's death (sorrow upon sorrow).

2:28 Therefore I am all the more eager to send him, so that when you see him again you may be glad and I may have less anxiety.

Because of the mutual feeling of Epaphroditus and the church for one another, and for Paul's own relief, Paul was "more eager." This and the next two verses could easily be understood to conceal some anxiety felt by Paul regarding the reception of Epaphroditus (cf. the discussion prior to v. 25). Thus he made his case as strongly as he did. Epaphroditus's return would produce a joy beyond the news he was well. "Less anxiety" (ἀλυπότερος, alypoteros) is from the same root as "sorrow" in verse 27.

2:29 Welcome him in the Lord with great joy, and honor men like him,

"In the Lord" picks up the words of verses 19 and 24. Paul may mean "welcome him as Christians should," manifesting the spirit of humility and service. "Honor" will be explained in the next verse. We presume there would be a welcome in any event, but Epaphroditus's dedication deserved special consideration. Note the joy language in this and the preceding verse. On joy see the notes at 1:4.

2:30 because he almost died for the work of Christ,

This verse is the climax of the passage, adding the final important details to Paul's praise of Epaphroditus and offering a word of inspiration to the readers. Not only did Epaphroditus do Christ's work as a bringer of the gift of love, but he also demonstrated the self-renouncing spirit so powerfully shown by Christ.

risking his life

No previous usage of the word translated "risked" (παρα–βολεύω, *paraboleuō*) has been discovered in any Greek text. One suggestion is that Paul employed a play on a gambling term. Epaphroditus risked for Christ's work, and won, because God had mercy. He did not let danger or hardship deter him from the task. It is even possible that the term may have implied some difficulties beyond the illness of Epaphroditus.

to make up for the help you could not give me.

Regarding the "help" (λειτουργία, *leitourgia*, the same Greek term as "take care" in v. 25) which had not been given, see 4:10,14,18. No criticism was implied in Paul's words. One has the sense of a messenger, commissioned with a great responsibility of love, determined to complete his mission, whatever the cost.

PHILIPPIANS 3

V. WARNING AGAINST "EVIL WORKERS" (3:1-3)

¹**Finally, my brothers, rejoice in the Lord! It is no trouble for me to write the same things to you again, and it is a safeguard for you. ²Watch out for those dogs, those men who do evil, those mutilators of the flesh. ³For it is we who are the circumcision, we who worship by the Spirit of God, who glory in Christ Jesus, and who put no confidence in the flesh —**

The letter now makes an abrupt and rather surprising turn. Matters are introduced of which there has been little, if any, forewarning. Not only does the content of the letter change, but the section we are now approaching offers certain stylistic peculiarities. "Finally" (v. 1) is understood by some as preparing for the conclusion of the letter (but see the notes on v. 1). If the reader skips from 3:1 to 4:4 the transition is a smooth one and there is no sense of loss of the intervening material. For this reason some have concluded 3:2–4:3 are an interpolated section — another writing of Paul inserted here.

There are other explanations of this phenomenon, however. Readers of Paul know that he can make abrupt shifts, sometimes even in midsentence (cf. Eph 3:1ff), though none are as extensive as this. Further, a personal letter does not flow like the development of a logical treatise. Changes of subject can be dramatic in such documents. There are also connections between 3:1-21 and 1:27-30, and the present text offers possible comment on the destruction and salvation statement of 1:28. If this section is a simple addition to the letter, why insert it here rather than near the end? And if the passage, though an interpolation, was meant to be understood as part of the original text, why wasn't it incorporated more smoothly into the text? Thus, the same argument that is used to favor an insertion can also argue against it.

As for the "finally" in verse 1, O'Brien argues a better sense is to understand it to mean "and so," as in 1 Thessalonians 4:1.[1] Thus it affords a transition, rather than introducing a conclusion. In 1 Thessalonians the word stands one third of the way from the end of the epistle.

3:1 Finally, my brothers, rejoice in the Lord!

Once again the call to joy is sounded (see the discussion at 1:4) but here for the first time "in the Lord" is added. Martin suggests this longer expression could be considered the equivalent of "hallelujah."[2] The last word (2:18) before the personal section in 2:19-30 was a like summons. Some, on the basis of the interpolation theory discussed above, wish to give "rejoice" the sense of "farewell." But the word does not appear in that sense elsewhere in the New Testament.

Here was joy despite potential problems. In fact the contexts in which joy is mentioned in Philippians always mention some difficulty.

It is no trouble for me to write the same things to you again, and it is a safeguard for you.

Paul knew the value of reminder and that a danger to faith could be simple forgetfulness, due to a lack of continual spiritual reflection and nourishment. The meaning of "write the same things" is problematic. Was a previous letter implied? Perhaps. Or was this the first time to write what had been previously delivered in some other form? What were the "same things?" Paul considered them a safeguard, so we think it may be both the multifaceted call to unity in the previous parts of the letter and the warnings which follow these words. They

---

[1]O'Brien, *Philippians*, p. 348.
[2]Ralph Martin, *Philippians* (Grand Rapids: Eerdmans, 1987), p. 138.

could even include the exhortation in 4:4-9. Note in 3:17f the
references to "example," "pattern," and to what was "often
told . . . before."

3:2 Watch out for those dogs, those men who do evil,

Even the casual reader is struck by Paul's abrupt change of
tone here. Various theories have been offered to explain it (an
interruption; a problem surfacing during the period the letter
was being dictated; stimulus from a coworker, perhaps Epaphroditus). This is a new problem, quite different from the previous text of the letter. To this point Paul had dealt primarily
with problems within the church. Here he seems to focus on
one from without. The description clearly indicates a threat
from a Jewish source. The attempt was to compel Christians to
observance of the law. The virulence of Paul's language has led
most writers to conclude these were evangelistic Jews (not
Christian) trying either to win back Jewish Christian converts or
to convert Gentile Christians. We should note, though, that
Paul could also use harsh language of Christian brothers whom
he opposed (cf. Gal 1:8f).

"Watch out" (βλέπετε, *blepete*) is repeated three times in the
Greek, giving a force the English lacks. The Greek also has
three words beginning with "k." They are the words translated
"dogs" (κύνας, *kynas*), "evil workers" (κακοὺς ἐργάτας, *kakous
ergatas*), and "mutilation" (κατατομήν, *katatomēn*). This
enhances the stylistic impact of the verse.

It seems better for us to consider Paul's words as a warning
of a possible danger than as a description of a problem within
the congregation. If the latter we would expect a more explicit indication of it.

"Dogs" get negative press throughout Scripture. Jews referred to Gentiles with this term, so Paul was apparently doing
a turn on that derogatory epithet in so referring to the Jews.
The strength of this "insult" is one reason for presuming Paul
did not speak of Judaizing Christians. "Those who do" translates a term used of Epaphroditus in 2:25 (in a compound
form — "fellow worker") and elsewhere of Christians. Other

translations render the term "workers." If Jews thought keeping the law made them good workers, Paul has done a turn on that as well. It was not that Paul saw law keeping as evil, but the intents of these people would deny salvation through Christ.

those mutilators of the flesh.

"Mutilators" seems an apparent play on circumcision. The word here is κατατομή (*katatomē*) and the word for circumcision is περιτομή (*peritomē*). The obvious Jewish coloring of this term is a reason for interpreting "dogs" and "men who do evil" in the Jewish sense. Paul had no argument against circumcision; indeed he had circumcised Timothy (Acts 16:3). It was the intent, not the act, that he opposed. Still, "mutilators" was a very strong term, and vividly conveyed Paul's distress (cf. Gal 5:12), no doubt caused by insistence this act was essential for salvation. It was not! It did not make one part of the new Israel. It was surgery, no more.

3:3 For it is we who are the circumcision,

Now Paul speaks of the true circumcision. It is described in three ways, as were those of whom Paul has just warned his readers. In other contexts Paul might simply have denied any need for circumcision as essential to salvation. But given this context it was an appropriate way to speak of God's true community. In a sense he said circumcision still marked the covenant people, if the term were properly understood.

we who worship by the Spirit of God,

The first mark of God's people was "worship by the Spirit of God."[3] Some see the next two terms as modifiers of this; i.e., such worship "glories in Christ" and "puts no confidence in the flesh." This does have the advantage of clarifying Paul's point. Otherwise it is hard to know just what point of difference from

---

[3]Because of a different Greek form for God some translations have the idea here of worshiping God. However the best manuscript evidence supports the reading in the NIV. See O'Brien, *Philippians*, p. 346 and Hawthorne, *Philippians*, p. 122.

Jewish worship he had in mind. Was he implying a contrast between ritual and a more spiritual worship (cf. John 2:24)?

Most commentators prefer to see these three terms as parallel. Then this would be worship by those indwelt by the Spirit and empowered by it in their lives of praise. The term λατρεύω (*latreuō*) translated "worship" is the Old Testament term for Israel's worship of God, used now by Paul of the new people of God.

who glory in Christ Jesus, and who put no confidence in the flesh —

"Glory" and "confidence" present two places the human heart can look for meaning and security. This is a theme Paul develops from his own experience in the next few verses. It is implied that Israel did not "glory in Christ Jesus" (obviously) and did put "confidence in the flesh." The verb translated "glory" (καυχάομαι, *kauchaomai*) is used by Paul thirty times in the New Testament, and only two times by other writers. We learn the meaning of "confidence in the flesh" from the following verses. To "glory in Christ Jesus" meant an abdication of pride in self and one's accomplishments. It admits the human need which, though real, is often ignored or disguised. The verb translated "put confidence" is found elsewhere in Philippians 1:6,14,25; and 2:25.

"Flesh" (σάρξ, *sarx*) is understood two ways in the commentaries. One position sees it as all in which humans trust; and the other as Jewish righteousness, with its lawkeeping, ritual, etc. Paul focuses on the second in the succeeding verses, but his case may have been a specific demonstration of a broader truth, i.e., the first meaning.

VI. PAUL'S CHANGED LIFE (3:4-11)

A. PAUL'S FORMER CONFIDENCE (3:4-6)

4though I myself have reasons for such confidence. If any-

one else thinks he has reasons to put confidence in the flesh, I have more: [5]circumcised on the eighth day, of the people of Israel, of the tribe of Benjamin, a Hebrew of Hebrews; in regard to the law, a Pharisee; [6]as for zeal, persecuting the church; as for legalistic righteousness, faultless.

Paul turns again to personal reference to enforce his point. He is arguing to support the true "circumcision" set forth in verse 3. In verses 4-6 he recounts his past, which would eminently qualify him for divine approval in the eyes of those against whom he inveighed in verse 2. His own situation made his point more telling than if he simply made impersonal arguments.

3:4 though I myself have reasons for such confidence.
Key words of this and the previous verse are "confidence" and "flesh." "Flesh" here was Paul's Jewishness, both by his birth status and by his personal accomplishments. But placing "confidence in the flesh" would be to lack ultimate confidence. Aside from the power of the argument *in context*, we are given marvelous insight into Paul's spiritual commitment (cf. also 2 Cor 11:16–12:11; Gal 1:13-24).

If anyone else thinks he has reasons to put confidence in the flesh, I have more:
This testimony would demonstrate to the reader that Paul knew whereof he spoke. He had once been on the other side of the fence, and knew the futility of that position. The wording of verse 2 showed how strongly he felt this. It is even possible that Paul may have presented his preeminence in Judaism as a way of saying "if I changed, so should others." Whoever would argue Paul changed because he was not a loyal and zealous Israelite would be refuted here.

3:5 circumcised on the eighth day, of the people of Israel,
This verse and the next list seven qualities. The first four were a result of birth and circumstance. The fifth, being "a

Pharisee," may have been a matter of heritage (cf. the son of a Pharisee in Acts 23:6) or of choice.

Several of these characteristics appear more significant if we assume that Paul was contrasting himself with Jewish proselytes. He was circumcised on the eighth day, in contrast to proselytes who would be circumcised later in life. "People" is from a word indicating racial descent, again in possible contrast to proselytes. Nor could a proselyte claim membership in a particular tribe, as Paul could (in Benjamin). And "Hebrew of Hebrews" may mean he spoke Hebrew and Aramaic, in distinction from Greek-speaking proselytes. It could also indicate his refusal to compromise with Greek culture (though compare his attitude in 1 Cor 9:19-23). But even if Paul was not making an implicit contrast here, his statements still supported his argument about the true source of righteousness. However, there was not any particular virtue in these first four items since they were Paul's "birthright," beyond his control.

of the tribe of Benjamin, a Hebrew of Hebrews;

Why the reference to Benjamin? Did this bear special significance in Judaism? Benjamin was the only son born in the promised land. Jerusalem was located in its tribal territory. The first king of Israel, Saul, was from Benjamin, and our Saul/Paul may have been named after him. Paul also noted that he was from Benjamin in Romans 11:1. Thus membership in this tribe seemed of special significance, though at this distance we may not know why.

in regard to the law, a Pharisee;

Besides this verse Pharisees are mentioned in the New Testament only in the Gospels and Acts. Their zeal for pure lives and rigid adherence to law and tradition is well known, as is the fact some of them carried it to excess (cf. the woes in Matt 23; Luke 11). They were admired by the people and many of them were admirable and energetic in their religious zeal (besides Paul, note Joseph of Arimathaea and Nicodemus).

95

3:6 as for zeal, persecuting the church;

Though zeal in normal Jewish thought might be understood as zeal for the law, Paul offers a surprising alternative. His former role as a persecutor was a lifelong haunting and, because of divine mercy, a source of joy (1 Cor 15:9; Gal 1:13, etc.). If he was convinced the church was so wrong, why did he change? This would seem to be an appeal to outsiders, not to Judaisers in the church. This could support the argument that Paul was opposing evangelistic non-Christian Jews.

as for legalistic righteousness, faultless.

"Legalistic" translates words which are literally "in law" (ἐν νόμῳ, *en nomō*), and the exact meaning of the term is debated. The most logical sense would be that they referred to one who achieved righteousness by law keeping. Is "legalistic" the best translation here? Does a modern negative attitude to the term unduly prejudice Paul's thought?

Paul was "faultless" (the Greek word, ἄμεμπτος [*amemptos*], is translated "blameless" in 2:15) in his law keeping. We believe one could observe the law's demands punctiliously and still come to have doubts, as Paul might have done even before the Damascus Road experience (cf. Acts 26:14). Some have felt a difficulty in reconciling "faultless" here with Paul's statements of failure in Romans 7:14-25 (assuming Romans describes his pre-Christian experience). It could well be, however, that Romans describes his inner perceptions, while the present text speaks of outward observance.

Bruce has well caught the thought of this and the next section when he observes that Paul "made the grade" only to find it inadequate![4]

B. FROM LOSS TO GAIN (3:7-11)

[7]But whatever was to my profit I now consider loss for the sake of Christ. [8]What is more, I consider everything a loss

---

[4]F.F. Bruce, *Philippians* (Peabody, MA: Hendrickson, 1983), p. 110.

compared to the surpassing greatness of knowing Christ Jesus my Lord, for whose sake I have lost all things. I consider them rubbish, that I may gain Christ [9]and be found in him, not having a righteousness of my own that comes from the law, but that which is through faith in Christ — the righteousness that comes from God and is by faith. [10]I want to know Christ and the power of his resurrection and the fellowship of sharing in his sufferings, becoming like him in his death, [11]and so, somehow, to attain to the resurrection from the dead.

3:7 But whatever was to my profit I now consider loss

Now Paul offers a striking personal contrast in validation of the situation described in verse 3. He employs bookkeeping language. "Profit" (κέρδος, *kerdos*) and "gain" (κερδαίνω, *kerdainō*, v. 8) describe the one side of the ledger, and "loss" (ζημία [*zēmia*], here and twice in v. 8) the other. The life transition was dramatic. "Profit" is a plural term, as if Paul had counted his past benefits one by one (like a miser, it has been suggested). But his mind changed ("consider") due to the powerful motivations which he relates in the following verses. "Loss" is singular, indicating all Paul once had was lumped together and put aside. The one who had measured his treasures individually now discards the whole stack of them as one.

for the sake of Christ.

Paul did not consider his background valueless *per se*. But in comparison to his new state, and as preferable to knowing Christ, it was "loss." Use of the term "rubbish" in verse 8 should be seen the same way — compared to Christ, and not as an absolute judgment. Upon analysis Paul counted as loss the saving value of correct ritual observance (circumcision), birth status (Israel, Benjamin, Hebrew of Hebrews) and personal accomplishments (Pharisees, zeal, law keeping).

3:8 What is more, I consider everything a loss

Paul now begins to amplify the statement of verse 7. In the

Greek verses 8-11 are a single sentence. He first develops the idea of loss, then goes on to speak of the profit, expanding the concept by speaking of what it means to "know" Christ. There is a powerful statement of divine grace in these verses. What Paul was and did was nothing. What Christ had done was everything. Nor was it just the Jewish background he counted loss. Paul gave his statement universal validity with the word "everything." Absolutely nothing could transcend for him the value of knowing Christ.

compared to the surpassing greatness of knowing Christ Jesus my Lord, for whose sake I have lost all things.

"Surpassing greatness" and "knowing" are in apposition — two ways of describing the same reality. The content of this experience is given in verses 9-11. "Knowing" here, therefore, included personal involvement — love, obedience and blessing. It was not just a detached intellectual awareness. Paul never knew Jesus in the flesh, though he did see him on the Damascus Road. But he *knew* him.

I consider them rubbish,

"Rubbish" (σκύβαλα, *skybala*) is a strong term, found only here in the New Testament. It has been called a vulgar word, and is the more forceful for that. A survey of the translations shows the variety of possibilities. They seem to fall into two categories. The word either refers to human waste or to unwanted food (garbage). Which of these two is meant here remains an object of discussion. With either option the point is unforgettable. Could Paul have put it any more strongly?

that I may gain Christ

"Gain" picks up the idea of "profit" from verse 7. The term indicates the "gain" experienced through life in relationship with Christ (cf. the idea of growth in Christ at 1:6; 2:13 and 16) as well as the ultimate gain at the last day. It goes from the Damascus Road to the final glory. The idea of growth will be further developed in verses 12ff.

3:9 and be found in him, not having a righteousness of my own that comes from the law, but that which is through faith in Christ — the righteousness that comes from God and is by faith.

Advancing on the idea of "surpassing greatness/knowing" the apostle now develops the idea of gaining Christ. It would involve righteousness (v. 9), power, sharing (v. 10), and the hope of resurrection from the dead (v. 11).

Some believe being found in Christ referred to the experiences of this life. Others see it as a hope for death. We believe it had a comprehensive meaning. The righteousness is God's gift in this life, but will assure acceptance by God at death.

There are two kinds of righteousness described here. The first, Paul says, is "of my own" and "comes from law." It represents human achievement, and writings like Galatians and Romans show how this righteousness cannot save. The second righteousness is "through faith in Christ," "comes from God," and is "by faith." It is quite possible that "faith in Christ" could mean the faithfulness of Christ. Christ's fidelity to God's purposes (cf. 2:5-11) achieved man's salvation. Then "by faith" in the last of the verse would refer to the human trust that must accept what God had done. This verse contrasts faith in Christ and human merit. If one attempts to receive righteousness by the latter means, then it cannot be gained by the former, which means, in Christian terms, it cannot be gained at all. Paul does not develop the reasons why righteousness that comes from the law is unavailing. Elsewhere he argued that law keeping imposed an impossible task (Gal 3:10ff).

3:10 I want to know Christ

The "knowing" of verse 8 is here elaborated as "power" (δύναμις, *dunamis*) and "fellowship" (κοινωνία, *koinōnia*) (the two expressions are preceded by a single article in Greek, unlike the English). Thus the knowledge was clearly experiential, depicting a lifestyle. Paul's expressed goal indicated his desire for continual progress, and is elaborated in verses 12-14.

and the power of his resurrection

"Power of his resurrection" probably did not mean Paul's resurrection, of which he speaks in the next verse. Rather the stress was on "power" — "power" so mighty that by it Jesus was victor over death. That power both energizes the life and sets its hope. In this context the special significance may be to the ability to endure suffering.

and the fellowship of sharing in his sufferings, becoming like him in his death,

"Sharing in his sufferings" does not imply that Paul sought martyrdom. "Sharing" (*koinōnia*) is the key word. To what does he refer by this and by the following reference to "death?" Some see these as referring to dying and rising in baptism. It seems preferable to consider the reference as the total experience of dying with Christ through life and accepting any consequences of that. To share with Christ is high joy and privilege to those with the assurance death cannot conquer them (cf. 1:29). The unbelievers would find Paul's words about suffering and death being gain highly puzzling. One only comes to glow with holy joy in the experience of faith.

3:11 and so, somehow, to attain to the resurrection from the dead.

The reference to resurrection here is clearly the final resurrection. The Greek expression, found only here, means something like "out of the death of the dead." "Attain" is a subjunctive, indicating something yet to be attained. Again the themes of the Christ hymn are seen as central to the letter, with these words echoing those of 2:8.

VII. PRESSING ON TO THE GOAL (3:12-16)

A. "ONE THING I DO" (3:12-14)

[12]Not that I have already obtained all this, or have already been made perfect, but I press on to take hold of that for

which Christ Jesus took hold of me. [13]Brothers, I do not consider myself yet to have taken hold of it. But one thing I do: Forgetting what is behind and straining toward what is ahead, [14]I press on toward the goal to win the prize for which God has called me heavenward in Christ Jesus.

Pulsing through these verses are the ideas of growth and progress in Christ, as well as the idea of spending maximum energy in the cause of Christ. The theme of growth permeates the letter (1:6,9-11, 2:1-4,12f, etc.) The idea of energy demonstrates that though righteousness comes by faith and is God's work, it does not imply a lax and indolent "let God do it" attitude (cf. 2:12f). The course to be run and the goal to be achieved are exciting and challenging, so that one who loves Christ because Christ loved him must run it.

But why are these words included here? Certainly Paul was using his own outlook as a way to encourage the readers to press on. Was there more? Parts of the text would make sense if we assume Paul was refuting those who claimed to have reached perfection (perhaps by lawkeeping, as v. 2 might imply). But if so, there are no other references to such persons in the book, and we might think Paul would be more explicit if he were debating them.

If it appeared from Paul's statements about "profit" and "loss" and "confidence in the flesh" that he seemed to deny the importance of human effort, his own testimony now refutes that.

3:12 Not that I have already obtained all this, or have already been made perfect,

Commentators have puzzled over what Paul had not "already attained." He had just spoken of knowledge of Christ, righteousness by faith, resurrection power, sharing in Christ's suffering and death, and future resurrection. He had already been accounted righteous, so that was probably not his meaning. Nor would it be the resurrection from the dead since he was discussing attainments in this life. Resurrection power and sharing with Christ could both be subsumed under "knowing Christ." Thus we suppose Paul spoke of further growth in Christ. He denies complacency and affirms yet unreached possibilities. Indeed, one of the joys of being in Christ is this process of open-ended growth. As one writer has observed, the more one knows of Christ the more one wishes to know. The opportunity opens before one like a race course. "Perfect" (from τελειόω, *teleioō*) is in parallel to "all this" and if Paul gave the term a different shade of meaning it is not clear from the text. Certainly these words would include an ethical dimension.

Those who think Paul was arguing against persons claiming to have reached perfection cite this passage (see the remarks above). "Perfect" implies the idea of completion or maturity, and need not be understood as complete sinlessness. The same term is rendered "mature" in verse 15.

but I press on to take hold of that for which Christ Jesus took hold of me.

Added to the power of the "loss" and "rubbish" images of verse 8 is the picture of a runner devoting maximum effort to finish the race. A runner would ignore all else in pursuit of "one thing" (v. 13). Christ took hold of Paul, which was grace, and Paul therefore pressed on, which was work responding to grace. God's deed was the motive. God allowed Paul to enter the race, but Paul had to run it.

3:13 Brothers, I do not consider myself yet to have taken hold of it.

The point must have been an important one, for Paul here affirmed his incompleteness a third time. Paul was doing more than giving a personal devotional statement. He was expressing what should be true for all Christians. Note that when he spoke of his Jewish background the idea was that he had "arrived." In Christ, however, he is "straining" forward. Yet the former gave no assurance, and the latter does.

But one thing I do: Forgetting what is behind and straining toward what is ahead,

Though a runner may occasionally steal a glance at competitors this dare not detract from the one goal of completing the race. Thus Paul forgot what was behind. This could include his achievements in Judaism as well as Christian accomplishments. Could it also include wrongs done, such as the persecution of the church? He was aware of these things but they did not weigh on him or deter his dedication. His forward progress was intense, as indicated by the strong "straining" (from ἐπεκτείνω, *epekteinō*). Cf. race imagery also in 1 Corinthians 9:24-27.

3:14 I press on toward the goal to win the prize for which God has called me heavenward in Christ Jesus.

This is a race in which all finishers are winners. Yet this does not diminish the effort of the runner, for the course (like a marathon) is such that even to finish is an achievement. The Greek term translated "goal" (σκοπός, *skopos*, literally "goal marker") is found only here in the New Testament. The prize is not defined, but would include all that is involved in complete fellowship with God beyond the restrictions encountered in this life. "Heavenward" (ἄνω, *anō*) does not translate the usual word for heaven, but is a term meaning "above" or "upwards." Some see the prize as identical to the call, and others as the reward. This kind of nuanced interpretation may oversophisticate a basic point which all Christians would understand quite well.

Hawthorne suggests an interesting interpretation, citing the custom of the herald announcing the name of the victor after the race (remember that in this race all finishers were winners).[5] Thus the image would be God calling the spiritual athlete and giving him the prize (in Christ) as his name was announced. This interpretation is colorful, though we cannot know if it was in Paul's mind or not.

---

[5]Hawthorne, *Philippians*, pp. 154f.

B. THE MATURE VIEWPOINT (3:15-16)

[15]All of us who are mature should take such a view of things. And if on some point you think differently, that too God will make clear to you. [16]Only let us live up to what we have already attained.

3:15 All of us who are mature

Paul now leaves his personal narrative to call readers to share the dedication he has expressed. If he was controverting those who claimed perfection (see discussion at v. 12), this could be his exhortation to them. They would be dealt with by God. But it has been argued that the gentleness of Paul's words here implies they were addressed to friends, not to opponents.

Not all would be "mature," so Paul was inviting those who lacked maturity to achieve it. It involved knowing the need to forget the past and press on. "Mature" is from the Greek word τέλειος (*teleios*) rendered "perfect" in verse 12. How are we to explain Paul's denial of the quality in verse 12 and his affirmation of it here? He may have been using the word in two senses, a not uncommon practice. In verse 12 it was the full knowledge of Christ, and here it was the recognition of one's incompleteness. Or Paul's use may have been ironical: i.e., the way to be perfect (mature) in Christ is to realize one is imperfect. "Grow up and recognize you aren't grown all the way yet." However Paul was using the terms, the ultimate call of the verse is clear.

should take such a view of things.

"Take . . . a view," as well as "think" both translate φρονέω (*phroneō*), a term often employed by Paul in this letter. See the discussion at 1:7. The term indicates the values of a lifestyle, not just intellectual concepts.

And if on some point you think differently,

The last sentence of this verse offers a major interpretive

problem. What is involved in "think differently"? The word for "think" (*phroneō*) would indicate it was not simply a matter of doctrine. Rather it would be belief which determined how one lived. Some think Paul now turns from major to minor issues, leaving it to God to convict those of whom he spoke. Others think he refers to the bad attitudes causing disunity in the church. In this case Paul felt that if he could not correct the division then he would let it be left to God. However, since disunity has always plagued the church, one would have to assume such correction would come at the last day. This implied threat of judgment does not seem to fit the tenor of Paul's argument here.

We prefer to think these were the immature who were not prepared to accept and practice the single-minded devotion to Christ which characterized Paul. Since ultimately it is God's active grace that leads to such commitment, Paul hoped that God would reveal the truth to them in ways that Paul's example could not. The apostle recognized that Christians are at different stages so he lovingly indicates how God leads each person to greater levels of Christian service and life. Paul himself knew he had growing to do, and thus did not grow impatient with others in the same condition. This was no bossy, "holier than thou" attitude.

that too God will make clear to you.

"Make clear" translates the verb (ἀποκαλύπτω, *apokalyptō*) from which "apocalyptic" and the Greek title for the book of Revelation come. The mode by which God would give revelation is not stated. Given the general use of the term in the New Testament, it is logical to hold that the revelation would come through the growing process of being Christian (as in fact it does for all Christians).

3:16 Only let us live up to what we have already attained.

This exhortation is corporate ("let us"). The mature and those who think differently should still follow Christ in unity, as would Paul himself. Differences in spiritual levels ought not deter Christians from being consistent with whatever level each had reached. Minor differences in spiritual development have often divided the church, and Paul would not have that happen in Philippi. "Already attained" would be the right-eousness that comes by faith and whatever of the blessings list-ed in verses 9-11 each had appropriated, though these things may not have exhausted Paul's intentions (cf. 1 Cor 4:17, and note "pattern" and "example" in the next verse). The apostle was apparently asking them to augment the growth process by building on what they had. Paul's words may indicate he feared apostasy or divisiveness by some.

VIII. TRUE AND FALSE MODELS (3:17-21)

[17]Join with others in following my example, brothers, and take note of those who live according to the pattern we gave you. [18]For, as I have often told you before and now say again even with tears, many live as enemies of the cross of Christ. [19]Their destiny is destruction, their god is their stomach, and their glory is in their shame. Their mind is on earthly things. [20]But our citizenship is in heaven. And we eagerly await a Savior from there, the Lord Jesus Christ, [21]who, by the power that enables him to bring everything under his control, will transform our lowly bodies so that they will be like his glori-ous body.

In this paragraph verse 17 gives a positive exhortation. Verses 18 and 19 describe a group negative to Christianity, and verses 20 and 21 the blessings of those committed to Christ.

3:17 Join with others in following my example, brothers, and take note of those who live according to the pattern we gave you.
"Example" and "pattern" are two ways of expressing the same thing. Paul taught the faith ("pattern") and also lived it.

In a day when no written New Testaments were available, it is possible the "incarnated" message was more influential than today (though not without influence in any age). It was important to follow Paul, however, only as he lived the pattern. Thus the deeper reality was to follow Christ. Throughout Philippians Paul has offered exhortation through example, with the Christ hymn (2:5-11) being the centerpiece. But Timothy and Epaphroditus were also commended for their examples.

Paul was no egotist here. He had expressed his renunciation of everything for Christ's sake in verses 7-11, and acknowledged his imperfection in verses 12-14. Indeed, these attitudes are basic to any who would follow Jesus. "Following" would be recognized by readers, however, as containing all those aspects of Paul's life and teaching which showed forth Christ.

"Join with others in following . . . example" (συμμιμητής, *symmimētēs*) translates an expression found only here in all Greek literature. The basic root, which means "mimic," is prefixed by "with." Quite possibly the prefix indicated that the "following" should be done together with one another — another stress on the importance of unity within the church.

"Pattern" (τύπος, *typos*) is singular, while "we" is obviously plural. Though some see a problem, we hold that the one pattern of Christian life was demonstrated by Paul, Timothy, and Epaphroditus, as they "mimicked" Christ. Some would change "we" to the singular, and argue that Paul was asserting apostolic authority. But this lacks textual support, and Paul was not concerned in this letter to affirm and defend his apostolicity (cf. absence of "apostle" in 1:1).

3:18 For, as I have often told you before and now say again even with tears,

Paul speaks of another facet of his past instruction — regarding the lamented enemies of the cross. "Often" indicates an intense and ongoing concern and probably a pervasive problem as well. There is no proof these people had reached Philippi. If they had not, they were yet perceived as a very real threat. Or previous warnings may not have been totally effective so that now they had infiltrated the church. We cannot know for sure. Paul's "tears" (cf. Acts 20:31; Rom 9:2f; 10:1; 2 Cor 2:4) indicate both his passionate personal concern and the seriousness of the situation. Imitation of Christ, then (v. 17), was a powerful antidote. Here and in verse 17 Paul has presented two ways to pursue, stressed by the repetition of "live."

many live as enemies of the cross of Christ.

Who were these people? Was their failing doctrinal or behavioral? Were they Christians or outsiders? A wide range of speculations has failed to resolve the question. If Christians, it has been suggested they may have been Judaizers; or perhaps quasi-Gnostics; or those who considered themselves outside any law; or those whose commitment was nominal; or those who denied Christ under persecution. If non-Christians, suppositions suggest heathens who opposed Christian ethical standards; or evangelistic Jews. Though the issue is very difficult, we think Paul's tears and the use of the word "enemies" (most significant if they might have been assumed to be friends) of the cross indicate Christians. Beyond this it is difficult to conjecture, but if a guess be hazarded, we would opt for Christians still snared in the ways of the world whose lifestyles evinced no true reform and who thus denied the efficacy of the cross for their lives. Whatever their reason for being in the church, it had little to do with God's intent in crucifixion. If this view be correct, we are not dealing with an organized party or position in the church but with moral failure. It may or may not have infected the Philippian church. A survey of the Pauline letters (and others in the New Testament) shows how pervasive was the problem of worldliness in the early church.

Another perspective on these people considers their relation to the "dogs," "evil men," and mutilators of verse two. If they were the same and those in verse 2 were Judaizers, then so were these. Though we have accepted an alternate view, we will show how this position leads us to understand the next verse.

3:19 Their destiny is destruction, their god is their stomach, and their glory is in their shame.

Those considering these as Judaizers interpret "stomach" as indicating the scrupulous practice of the food laws; in Paul's view virtually deifying them. "Shame," which is a term for the private organs, is interpreted as circumcision, with the sense that they boasted because of their circumcision. Though Paul says nothing against circumcision *per se* (see the notes on 3:3) in this context it was shameful to him because they gloried in it.

If these were worldly Christians then the "stomach" could refer to gluttony in the specific sense, or to unlicensed sensuality in the more general sense. Thus "stomach" would stand for all uncontrolled appetites. And "shame" would refer to excesses as well, especially of a sexual nature.

Where did this course lead? Inevitably to destruction and thus to the opposite destiny from that which God intended for humans. Some suggest "destruction," "stomach," and "shame" all implied the perishability of man. Thus these people had given the highest value to that which must pass away. This was a sad situation indeed. No wonder Paul wept.

Their mind is on earthly things.

"Mind" is from another form of *phroneō* (see the notes at 1:7). This was their life intent and direction. "Earthly things" (ἐπίγεια, *epigeia*) forms a sad counterpoint to "heaven" in the next verse.

3:20 But our citizenship is in heaven.

As Paul contrasted his past (and Jewish achievements) with his present in verses 4-11, so here he completes another contrast of lifestyles. A link is formed to verses 20 and 21 by verse 11. The resurrection noted there receives fuller elaboration here.

Verses 20 and 21 form a contrast to verses 18 and 19 in several ways. The "mind on earthly things" contrasts with "heavenly citizenship." The "stomach as god" contrasts with the transformation of the body to be like Christ's. And "glory in shame" contrasts with likeness to Christ's glorious body.

Because of the language, form, and theology of this section some have conjectured it was also a Christian hymn, as was 2:5-11. Others disagree, but grant that the verses may contain hymnic fragments. Still others think the un-Pauline expressions may be because the apostle reflected earlier Christian traditional usage.

Morna Hooker has observed an interesting relation of these verses to 2:5-11. Verses 5-8 of chapter 2 speak of Christ becoming like man; verses 9-11 speak of him as he now is; and the present text speaks of men as they will be when transformed into his likeness.[6]

"Citizenship" (πολίτευμα, *politeuma*) translates a word found nowhere else in the New Testament. The parallel is probably to the right of Roman citizenship possessed by the citizens of Philippi. Wherever a Philippian went, he enjoyed the "rights and privileges" of his Roman citizenship, and he would spread Roman culture as well. So those in Christ, wherever they were, and whatever their circumstances, were heavenly citizens. Included in that position was the assurance of a wonderful transformation. What a powerfully sustaining thought! The Christian thus possessed both present and future blessing. See Hebrews 11:13,16; and 1 Peter 1:4f.

And we eagerly await a Savior from there, the Lord Jesus Christ,

"Enemies of the cross" denied the saving efficacy of the crucifixion. By contrast his followers acknowledge Christ as Savior (the first time Paul adds the term to Jesus' name in Philippians). Because Jesus had saved and would save their lives, they knew the excited anticipation of "eagerly" awaiting.

3:21 who, by the power that enables him to bring everything under his control,

The certainty of that which Paul anticipated is underscored by the reference to power. Though "power" (ἐνέργεια, *energeia*)

---

[6]Cited in Bruce, *Philippians*, p. 135.

could be described with several illustrations, this is the ultimate one, comprehending all others. The word "power"
comes from a Greek root which stands behind the English
"energy."

will transform our lowly bodies

"Lowly" (ταπεινώσις [tapeinōsis]; some translations have
"vile") was not meant to derogate the body, but to indicate its
weakness or frailty. But God who raises the dead brings
strength out of weakness. The Christian doctrine is the resurrection and transformation of the body. It will be changed, as
Paul said in 1 Corinthians 15:44, to a spiritual body (see 1 Corinthians 15:42ff for the fullest description of the phenomenon
in the New Testament). Similar ideas are found in 2 Corinthians 4:16–5:4 and 1 John 3:2. The enemies focused on the
body only as it related to this life (v. 19). Christ called men to
consider it as it related to the next. The Christian's destiny is
not decay, but transformation.

so that they will be like his glorious body.

"Like his glorious body," though an expression incapable of
exact definition, sets the mind stretching to exalted heights,
and raises hope to the boiling point.

PHILIPPIANS 4

IX. EXHORTATIONS TO STEADFASTNESS, UNITY, PRAYER, AND PROPER THOUGHT (4:1-9)

A. STANDING FIRM (4:1)

¹Therefore, my brothers, you whom I love and long for, my joy and crown, that is how you should stand firm in the Lord, dear friends!

The NIV puts this verse with the end of chapter 3. Since it appears to be transitional in nature, it is debated whether it concludes the preceding section or introduces what follows. Perhaps it was meant to serve both functions, indicating the need to "stand firm" because of what being "in the Lord" meant and to "stand firm" in the ways to be subsequently elaborated.

4:1 Therefore, my brothers, you whom I love and long for,
Paul's strong expression of affection for his readers in 1:7, 8 is surpassed here. He refers to them six ways in this verse, and the combined effect is moving indeed. Whatever their problems they had not diminished Paul's care for them.

my joy and crown, that is how you should stand firm in the Lord, dear friends!
"Joy" again sounds the note heard often in this letter (cf. notes on 1:4). "Crown" (στέφανος, *stephanos*) is not the royal crown (diadem) but could either refer to a victor's wreath at the games or to the garland placed on a guest at a banquet.

Was Paul thinking of the joy of a feast or of the joy of a victory?
The same term is used in 2 Timothy 4:8. "In the Lord" is an
expression that was found in 2:19,24,29; and 3:1; and will be
found in 4:2,4 and 10 (see the notes at 2:29; 3:1). The expression could mean "stand firm" as Christians should or "stand
firm" as empowered by God. The possible military implications
of the Greek could be especially relevant in Philippi, since many
of the inhabitants were from families with military experience.

B. EUODIA AND SYNTYCHE (4:2-3)

**²I plead with Euodia and I plead with Syntyche to agree
with each other in the Lord. ³Yes, and I ask you, loyal yokefellow,ᵃ help these women who have contended at my side in
the cause of the gospel, along with Clement and the rest of
my fellow workers, whose names are in the book of life.**

ᵃ2 Or *loyal Syzygus*

Verses 2-9 offer specific and very personal instructions. The
call to unity addressed to two women (vv. 2, 3) continues the
emphasis of 1:27; 2:1-11,14-16; and 3:16. The exhortation to
joy (v. 4) echoes a frequently heard theme (cf. notes at 1:4).
Gentleness (v. 5) also was essential to oneness in the church
(cf. 2:1-4). Anxiety (vv. 6f) could well be a cause of division,
and was a perspective to be combatted by peace-producing
prayer. The call to appropriate thinking (vv. 8,9) reflects the
many references to proper thought in the book (cf. 1:9-11; 2:1-
4 and uses of φρονέω [*phroneō*] listed at notes to 1:7). Paul's
teaching and practice (v. 9) catch up most of his statements,
but notice particularly 3:17. Therefore verses 2-9, which some
have considered discrete and unrelated exhortations, really fit
neatly into the conceptual fabric of this letter.

4:2 I plead with Euodia and I plead with Syntyche to agree
with each other in the Lord.
Imagine the reaction when this letter was read aloud to the

church and two women, presumably present, were singled out! This is the first time the epistle becomes this specific. There are various theories, but we believe Paul wished to build the foundation for his plea throughout the letter before coming to the specific application. His previous words would make this appeal the more irresistible.

How important were these women? Some consider them minor. We do know that a prominent woman was converted to begin the Philippian church (Lydia, Acts 16). We would suggest, from the very fact these names were specified, and from the supporting words of verse 3, that they had significant influence in the church and may have been at the very center of the disunity discussed throughout the letter. If they were not a center of the problem, why didn't Paul mention the ones who were? One suggestion has been that their homes may have afforded meeting places for the church. Some have tried to identify Euodia with Lydia, but this theory has strained the linguistic similarities and has not won consent. Paul appealed to both equally, avoiding any hint of favoritism. The word "agree" is another use of *phroneō* and refers to aims and attitudes, not just consensus on some point of doctrine or disagreement. Paul urged a unity of spirit, not a grudging and irritated compromise. The same language was applied to the church in 2:2.

"In the Lord" is found here, as it was in verse 1. Did it mean "by the Lord's power" or "as Christians should?"

4:3 Yes, and I ask you, loyal yokefellow,

A situation is understood more fully the more one knows about the persons involved. So those who first read this letter could infer much detail that we are denied. As Euodia and Syntyche remain somewhat mysterious to us, so here we have "loyal yokefellow," Clement, and "fellow workers," all of whom are no more than names or descriptions, limited to what this verse tells us. "Loyal yokefellow" was the helper, perhaps summoned specifically because of skills as a peacemaker (was he a man of prayer, guarded by peace — vv. 6f?) "Yokefellow" translates the Greek σύζυγε (*syzyge*, the vocative form of *syzygos*), which might possibly be a proper name. If so, "loyal" could be Paul's way of indicating Syzygus was truly what he was named. Other views as to his identity have ranged through Epaphroditus, Timothy, Silas, Luke, and some even contend this was a collective term for the entire church (a view O'Brien dubs "unusual").[1]

help these women who have contended at my side in the cause of the gospel,

Euodia and Syntyche had been Paul's allies in contending for the gospel. The word translated "contend" (συναθλέω, *synathleō*) was also in 1:27. From the Greek comes our word "athlete." The intensity implied by this word indicates that their division had diminished the impact of "fighting the good fight."

along with Clement and the rest of my fellow workers, whose names are in the book of life.

Clement and "the fellow workers" also remain an enigma. The latter term may be used because there were too many to name individually. On the background of the "book of life" see Exodus 32:32; Psalm 69:28 and Isaiah 4:3. Some argue the term had special meaning beyond the eternal life possessed by all believers, as if to say to those who have eternal life that they were not necessarily in the book of life. If that was the meaning, it is difficult to know what the special meaning might have been. It seems strange that Paul would imply some distinction, especially when "book of life" seems, in the passages cited, to refer to God's covenantal people, and not to some special class within that category. The fact that Paul complements these fellow workers in this way need not demand such an exclusivistic meaning. See also Revelation 3:5; 20:15 and 21:27.

---

[1]O'Brien, *Philippians*, p. 481.

C. JOY, PRAYER, PEACE (4:4-7)

[4]**Rejoice in the Lord always. I will say it again: Rejoice!** [5]**Let your gentleness be evident to all. The Lord is near.** [6]**Do not be anxious about anything, but in everything, by prayer and petition, with thanksgiving, present your requests to God.** [7]**And the peace of God, which transcends all understanding, will guard your hearts and your minds in Christ Jesus.**

4:4 Rejoice in the Lord always. I will say it again: Rejoice!

Because this verse repeats the words of 3:1 it has been conjectured that the intervening verses may have been interjected into the original letter. See the discussion at 3:1. Discussion of this dual exhortation centers on its relation to the rest of the paragraph. Grammatically it stands alone. Was it a statement separate from verses 5-7, or are the matters discussed there to be taken as consequences of joy? Thematically joy can certainly be connected with gentleness, with the nearness of the Lord, and with prayer and peace. Thus that may be the intent here. A "joyless" religion would hardly be of the sort described in the following verses.

This great summons to joy catches up another thread that runs through the letter (cf. the notes at 1:4). It seems most likely Paul saw joy as a key to resolving the Philippian problems, and thus he introduces the idea so frequently.

"In the Lord" is found for the third time in four verses (see vv. 1,2). See the previous discussions for possible meanings. Relation to the Lord gives both reason and power to rejoice.

"Rejoice" (χαίρετε, *chairete*) could also be translated "farewell," and this view is favored by those seeing 3:2–4:3 as an insertion. But "always" indicates a continual practice, and thus goes beyond the limits that would be supposed by "farewell."

4:5 Let your gentleness be evident to all.

"Gentleness" (ἐπιεικές, *epieikes*) refers to a gracious and reasonable spirit. In particular it forsakes insistence on one's own rights in order to benefit others. Once more the centrality of the Christ hymn (2:5-11) in displaying this spirit should be noticed. The relation of this view of things to resolving discord in the church is obvious. A gentle person would even be willing to bear unpleasant treatment if that were warranted. This was not a cowed attitude, showing lack of courage. Rather it was a response of strength, inspired by the relation to Christ.

The Lord is near.

"The Lord is near" gives reason for rejoicing and for possessing gentleness. The expression may indicate nearness in terms of personal relationship. Thus all would be done with a sense of Christ's fellowship and empowering. Others think the term may refer to the Lord's return, which the early church expected to occur at any time (as the church should in any age). This view relates to previous references in the epistle to the day of the Lord (cf. 1:6,10,23; 2:10,16f; 3:8). Paul did not know the exact time of the parousia, but he knew history was under God's control and would serve God's ultimate purposes. Thus one should act as God willed within history. Of course Christ did not come during Paul's life, but his words, on this interpretation, serve as reminders that Christians live between the two comings of Jesus.

It is possible that we have here an intentional double meaning. The Lord who was near to care and help could also return at any time.

4:6 Do not be anxious about anything, but in everything, by prayer and petition,

Anxiety can produce irritability and defensiveness. It is a soil in which discord could grow. Indeed matters that might otherwise be of lesser moment can reach swollen proportions when fed by anxiety. The verb here rendered "be anxious" (μεριμνάω, *merimnaō*) is translated "take interest" in 2:20. Though anxiety is not specifically addressed elsewhere in the letter, it could clearly be both a cause of and a consequence of the situation in the Philippian church. "Stop worrying" is the literal meaning, and was more than just a negative commandment.

Paul gave a way to stop. As he had often used "in the Lord" to indicate the special way Christ impacted the Christian's life, so here prayer is specified (cf. 1:3-11,19). Three prayer terms are used in this verse (prayer, petition, requests). Let God's power address men's concern. If divine power could not effect resolution, then none would be possible. That would be cause for worry! And prayer is as wide as life, for "everything" is its scope.

with thanksgiving, present your requests to God.
"Thanksgiving" (εὐχαριστία, *eucharistia*) recognized God's blessings and control of circumstances. Anxiety tends to forget God, to rely on human resources. So both prayer and a recognition of God's love and goodness are powerful, and together they are most effective. Recall God is the God who urges men to pray (Luke 11:9-13). Will their self-centeredness turn them away from real help?

4:7 And the peace of God,
For a troubled church "peace" (εἰρήνη, *eirēnē*) was the divine promise. Even if specific prayers were not answered, peace still comes to the believer. The image is of a soldier standing guard, which would be particularly relevant in Philippi, a city protected by a Roman garrison. Anxiety is denied admittance to a heart and mind so guarded.

This is the only New Testament occurrence of the expression "peace of God." More than the peace God gives, it is the peace which God *is*. God gives, and Christians receive, something of himself.

which transcends all understanding,
Paul often recognized how divine realities soar beyond even the most exalted human conception. "Transcends understanding" expresses such a case. Interpretations of his meaning suggest, in addition to that which is beyond human comprehension, the idea that such peace was better than any human planning or schemes could produce. But if one of these was his meaning, so must the other be.

119

will guard your hearts and your minds in Christ Jesus.

"Hearts and minds" indicates the entire inner person, and feeds into the discussion of thought in the next paragraph. "In Christ Jesus" corresponds to "in the Lord" in verses 1, 2, and 4.

D. THINK AND DO (4:8-9)

[8]**Finally, brothers, whatever is true, whatever is noble, whatever is right, whatever is pure, whatever is lovely, whatever is admirable — if anything is excellent or praiseworthy — think about such things.** [9]**Whatever you have learned or received or heard from me, or seen in me — put it into practice. And the God of peace will be with you.**

4:8 Finally, brothers,

Paul, who liked lists, concludes this series of exhortations with one. This one contains eight items — six ethical qualities followed by two summary words. The unusual thing about it is that two of these eight qualities are mentioned nowhere else in the New Testament; another is elsewhere only in the Pastorals, and still another is nowhere else in Paul's writings. Since many of these terms are found in lists of virtues used by non-Christian moralists of the day, it is possible Paul was depicting the best of pagan thought and holding it up for Christian consideration. The fact that Paul used these terms, however, does not mean he endorsed the non-Christian background in which they were set. To the Greek mind these virtues were philosophical, not religious. Paul reoriented them by setting them in a Christian context.

Philippians never quotes the Old Testament, though there are allusions. So the apostle appeals to these brethren out of their own Gentile background. This shows how non-Christian material could be "baptized" for Christian use, and how Paul was "all things to all men."

This verse calls for thought and reflection, and the next for action. "Don't just ponder, but do." Perhaps Paul was indicating that these were the peace-producing attitudes, if observed "in Christ Jesus."

With "finally" the verse begins with wording very similar to 3:1. "Finally" concludes Paul's list of exhortations. Then after a personal section Paul will conclude the letter.

whatever is true, whatever is noble, whatever is right, whatever is pure, whatever is lovely, whatever is admirable —

The Greek syntax gives each of the first six virtues distinct emphasis. "True" (ἀληθής, *alēthēs*) indicated that one's thoughts conformed to reality. This was not truth reached as the end of a logical thought process, as much as truthfulness; i.e., integrity and reliability of character. The Greek term for "noble" (σεμνός, *semnos*) is translated in various ways. It referred to lofty things, honorable, worthy of respect. Thought should not center on the cheap and vulgar. "Right" (δίκαιος, *dikaios*) means to be just, both with regard to men and in obeying the divine standard. "Pure" (ἁγνός, *hagnos*) has to do with proper motives, free from sin, and, in the Christian sense, centered on God. "Lovely" (προσφιλής, *prosphilēs*) is a word found only here in the New Testament, nor was it used as a virtue in any ancient text. It referred to that which was lovable by its nature. "Admirable" (εὔφημος, *euphēmos*) is also unique here in the New Testament. Plummer defines it as that which is kind and winning, not offensive.

if anything is excellent or praiseworthy —

"Excellent" (ἀρετής, *aretēs*) translates a term which in Stoic philosophy described man's highest goal and true destiny. So Paul paraded all moral excellencies before his readers for consideration. These summary terms ("excellent," "praiseworthy") comprehended the entire scope of proper thought, since listing every possible attitude would tax both writer and reader.

think about such things.

Here again the faith is centered in the human thought process; in its values and view of life. Throughout the letter this has been stressed (cf. notes at 1:7).

4:9 Whatever you have learned or received or heard from me, or seen in me — put it into practice.

Now the call was to action ("do"). Four verbs describe what was communicated to the Philippians. The last ("seen") referred to Paul's own life (cf. 3:17). "Heard," if it refers to what they had heard of his life and character, may have had the same sense. "Learned" or "received" probably referred to his teaching, and "heard" may also. He had just listed pagan virtues with Christian implications. "Learned" may imply specific Christian instruction beyond that. "Receive" (παραλαμβάνω, *paralambanō*) was a term frequently used of passing on of a tradition (1 Cor 11:23; 15:1-5; Gal 1:9; Col 2:6; 1 Thess 4:1ff; 2 Thess 2:15; and 3:16ff). Since the admonition was to Christian practice we may presume all four terms deal with ethical Christian behavior.

And the God of peace will be with you.

The "peace of God" (v. 7) is now complemented with the "God of peace." In this case the reference is to God himself producing peace through the qualities in verse 8 and those implied by verse 9. Cf. on the expression Romans 15:33; 16:20; 1 Corinthians 13:11; and 1 Thessalonians 5:23. Again we see the appropriateness of the description of the blessing to needs created by the Philippian discord.

One might see verses 2-8 as steps to be taken to cure division within the church. They would be rejoicing, gentleness, prayer and thanks, proper thought and proper action.

X. RESPONSE TO THE PHILIPPIANS' GENEROSITY (4:10-20)

[10]**I rejoice greatly in the Lord that at last you have renewed your concern for me. Indeed, you have been concerned, but you had no opportunity to show it. [11]I am not saying this because I am in need, for I have learned to be content whatever the circumstances. [12]I know what it is to be in need, and**

I know what it is to have plenty. I have learned the secret of being content in any and every situation, whether well fed or hungry, whether living in plenty or in want. [13]I can do everything through him who gives me strength. [14]Yet it was good of you to share in my troubles. [15]Moreover, as you Philippians know, in the early days of your acquaintance with the gospel, when I set out from Macedonia, not one church shared with me in the matter of giving and receiving, except you only; [16]for even when I was in Thessalonica, you sent me aid again and again when I was in need. [17]Not that I am looking for a gift, but I am looking for what may be credited to your account. [18]I have received full payment and even more; I am amply supplied, now that I have received from Epaphroditus the gifts you sent. They are a fragrant offering, an acceptable sacrifice, pleasing to God. [19]And my God will meet all your needs according to his glorious riches in Christ Jesus. [20]To our God and Father be glory for ever and ever. Amen.

In a final personal section Paul discusses gifts he had been sent by the Philippians. In receiving them Paul seems to have suspended his usual policy of not calling upon the churches for support (1 Cor 4:8-13; 9:12; 2 Cor 11:7-10; 1 Thess 2:5-12; 2 Thess 3:7-12). However, Ralph Martin has argued, on the basis of 1 Corinthians 9:15-27 and 2 Corinthians 11:9 that Paul did take help from others, and Holmberg argues Corinth was the exception; i.e., they were the only church from which he would not accept help.

Two motifs run through these verses. First was appreciation for their concern (vv. 10,14-16 and 18-20) and the other was affirmation of his confidence in God's gift of inner contentment in any circumstance (vv. 11-13,17). Because the language is more formal than elsewhere in the letter some think Paul wrote with some embarrassment. He was grateful, but he had learned to get along even without their help. This view also notes that Paul nowhere used the word for "give thanks" in this discussion — leading to the description "a thankless thanks" for this section. Thus there was something of a tension in Paul's joyful response. He was glad, especially for the blessing that giving had been for them (vv. 17f), but he could also have survived even without their help.

This is a possible interpretation. But it is also possible that Paul was using his own case for hortatory purposes, as elsewhere in the letter. His ultimate trust was in God for contentment, and he would have had this regardless. This would, however, have been an inner attitude, and would not have filled his stomach or met his material needs. Thus one who was content while hungry or in want would still appreciate help with food or with whatever else was required. Of course we are not told the nature of the gifts, but nothing is more logical than to assume they were material. Did he need food, clothing, medicine, money? We do not know.

One also wonders why this discussion comes at the very end of the letter. If Paul was expressing a "thankless thanks" he may have wished to delay discussion of such a delicate matter as long as possible. Others have thought that Paul may have waited till he was through dictating in order to write these personal remarks with his own hand. Though this expression of joy was one reason Paul wrote to the church, it may have been an aside from his main point(s) — concern for unity, false teachers (3:2), and enemies of the cross (3:18). Thus he could delay it because it was an item of lesser importance.

4:10 I rejoice greatly in the Lord that at last you have renewed your concern for me.

We see again the familiar "rejoice . . . in the Lord" (cf. 3:1; 4:4) so that here Paul did himself what he had previously exhorted his brethren to do. His joy was both for present and past concern. The Greek translated "renewed" (ἀνεθάλετε, *anethalete*) occurs nowhere else in the New Testament, but elsewhere describes a bush or tree budding in the spring. It was a lovely image for their concern. "Concern" and "concerned" are the last two uses of *phroneō* in the book (see discussion 1:7).

Indeed, you have been concerned, but you had no opportunity to show it.

Why had the Philippians had no opportunity to help Paul? Many suggestions have been made, some explaining the words in terms of the situation in Philippi, and some in terms of Paul's situation. In the former category conjectures include poverty, or lack of funds due to their gifts to Jerusalem (2 Cor 8:1-5), or lack of a messenger. Regarding Paul's situation some say he may have had no need, or that he discouraged help because he had formerly been criticized (1 Thess 2:9; 2 Thess 3:7-10; 1 Cor 9:3-18; 2 Cor 12:13-18), or that he was in an inaccessible place. Neither do we know how Paul knew the Philippians had been concerned during the time help had not been forthcoming.

4:11 I am not saying this because I am in need,

Understanding of this verse depends on what Paul meant by "need" and by "content." The latter term described a situation independent of life's physical circumstances, as verse 12 shows. So, if "need" was the opposite of "content" then Paul said he had the resources necessary for inner security. Possibly "need" could be understood in two senses. There were the outward necessities, which Paul might well need, if the Philippians had read his situation aright. But there was also an inner dimension, which is what Paul meant here. In other words, he had conquered anxiety, just as he exhorted his brethren to do (v. 6). So Paul could use the gift in the physical sense, but he had inner peace even without physical provision. He was not eagerly pacing his cell, asking every five minutes if the mail had come, as Craddock cleverly puts it.[2]

for I have learned to be content whatever the circumstances.

Paul could be saying these words to allay any concerns of the Philippians over his welfare while they had no opportunity to help. Even if he had been hungry (v. 12 could be read to

---

[2]Craddock, *Philippians*, p. 178.

imply this), he was all right because of an inner strength. This contentment did not come automatically, but had to be "learned." Possibly the lesson first broke on him at his conversion and was strengthened from that point on. Nor are we told how he learned this, but an understanding of the genius of life in Christ combined with Paul's crisis-riddled career leads to the conclusion that Paul would have had to learn this lesson to survive.

The word rendered "content" (αὐτάρκης, *autarkēs*) is only here in the New Testament, though cognates are found in 1 Corinthians 9:8 and 1 Timothy 6:6. Philosophers used the word to describe the independence wisdom brought. Paul changed the idea into an independence of dependence — on Christ.

4:12 I know what it is to be in need, and I know what it is to have plenty. I have learned the secret of being content in any and every situation, whether well fed or hungry, whether living in plenty or in want.

Now Paul elaborates on "circumstances" of verse 11. He had acquired two kinds of knowledge: first, of need and plenty; and second, of being content. Any survey of Paul's life can amply document need and hunger (cf. 1 Cor 4:11; 2 Cor 11:27). "Plenty" and "well fed" might even refer to his pre-Christian life (cf. 3:4b-6) but we need not suppose his Christian experience was always one of deprivation.

"Need" renders a term (ταπεινόω, *tapeinoō*) with the basic meaning of being humbled. Usually the opposite term meant "exalted." Sometimes Paul was humbled by circumstance and other times he imposed humiliation on himself — in either case for the sake of Christ and in imitation of him (cf. 2:8). To the outsider, overly concerned with material things, Paul's seeming nonchalance and inner calm would appear as a mystery or "secret." Paul's attitude toward food might be contrasted with those whose "god" was "the stomach" (3:19).

4:13 I can do everything through him who gives me strength.

How could a man whose stomach was pinched from hunger

and who suffered other deprivations exude joy, rather than whining complaint? It was because of inner power, here expressed in one of the favorite devotional texts of the New Testament. He took no credit for a bright attitude, but gave God the glory in "any and every" situation.

This verse is often misapplied, though with good intentions. Paul's statement must be understood in context. "Any and every" is not a universal statement, suggesting that anything in all of life can be done by God's power. Of course that power is without limit, but there are things God did not and does not intend to do, such as removing Paul's thorn in the flesh (2 Cor 12:7-9). We must see that Paul spoke here of the secret of contentment. Whenever the gift is utilized, even in the grimmest circumstances, it is by divine strength. This was no humanistic "feel good, regardless" philosophy.

4:14 Yet it was good of you to share in my troubles.

The gift was not necessary for Paul's contentment, but was still appreciated. The wonder of divine help is inestimable, but Paul still appreciated the love of God in human form, i.e., in the Philippians. Though content in hunger and need, one should not assume Paul would choose these states over having plenty and being well fed. Thus the gift was appreciated, but so was the Christlike attitude of the Philippians. His commendation was fulsome, not grudging. "Share" (συγκοινωνέω, *synkoinōneō*) is from a word group found also in 1:5,7; 2:1; 3:10 and 4:15 (cf. notes at 1:5). The sharing was not just in Paul's personal situation, but sharing in the spreading of the message of Christ.

4:15 Moreover, as you Philippians know, in the early days of your acquaintance with the gospel, when I set out from Macedonia, not one church shared with me in the matter of giving and receiving, except you only;

Now Paul reviews the previous generosity of the Philippians toward him, as if to compliment them for once more showing their loving and generous spirit. Some commentators, drawing from Paul's statements in verses 17 and 18, think Paul was less than enthusiastic and perhaps even exasperated with the Philippians. In their view he was saying "it was kind and good of you, but I really didn't need it, and don't need any more." This view we hold to be incorrect, presenting a problem which does not seem to reflect what we consider a more natural reading of the text. Yet the inquiring Bible student should at least investigate this perspective.

In the past Paul had been willing to receive help, both when he was in Thessalonica (v. 16 — at least twice) and later ("when I set out from Macedonia"). Some say "you know" should be understood as Paul's way of saying they had amply demonstrated their love for him, and no more was needed. We think it is not that, but a grateful way of affirming that they had always cared.

"Philippians" translates an unusual form (Φιλιππήσιοι, *Philippēsioi*), Latin in character, and Paul probably used it out of respect for the character of their city and their Roman citizenship. "Giving and receiving" (δόσις, *dosis*, and λῆμψις, *lēmpsis*) are commercial terms, but beyond that signify special friendship.

An interpretive problem centers in "in the early days of your acquaintance." The words are literally "in the beginning" of the gospel. "Of your acquaintance" is an interpretive addition in the NIV. The beginning of Paul's preaching was not in Macedonia, but he may have meant the beginning of his preaching there (cf. 1:3-5, especially 4) rather than in the broader sense of his entire preaching career. Another dilemma is whether "set out from Macedonia" means when he first left there (for Corinth) or after he had left there. This latter interpretation relates well to 2 Corinthians 11:8, which indicates he received support from "other churches" while in Corinth. Could it have been brought by Silas and Timothy (Acts 18:5) as Bruce suggests?

4:16 for even when I was in Thessalonica, you sent me aid again and again when I was in need.

If verse 15 referred to help sent to Corinth, now Paul

recalls an earlier example of generosity. The language could be understood of Thessalonica as well as of other places. Their help followed Paul on his travels, showing constant concern. Paul went to Thessalonica soon after leaving Philippi, so their care did not tarry. Acts 17:2 indicates Paul was in Thessalonica three weeks. Soon after he left he wrote 1 and 2 Thessalonians, in which he made no reference to help from Philippi. Contrariwise, he said he worked for his support (1 Thess 2:9; 2 Thess 3:8). Was the help inadequate for his needs, or was the help sent once the Philippians became aware of Paul's needs, toward the end of his stay? If we consider the language as implying other places, help may have been sent as he left and then subsequently (Berea?). Some feel these circumstances suggest a stay in Thessalonica of more than three weeks. If so, this must be squared with Acts 17:2, which says Paul argued in the synagogues for three weeks, and Acts 17:10, which says the brethren "immediately" sent Paul and Silas away by night. Perhaps the events of Acts 17:4,5 could allow for more time.

4:17 Not that I am looking for a gift, but I am looking for what may be credited to your account.

The first part of this verse parallels verse 11. In the second part Paul addresses the benefit of the gift to the givers, which connects to his blessing on them in verse 19. Paul's words show they had not given because pressured by him to do so. Their free response made their generosity the more admirable, for in so doing they emulated Jesus, who gave himself. "Credited to your account" (πλεονάζοντα εἰς λόγον ὑμῶν, *pleonazonta eis logon hymōn*) is another commercial term (see notes on v. 15). That which was credited was their fruit — the literal meaning of "what."

4:18 I have received full payment and even more; I am amply supplied, now that I have received from Epaphroditus the gifts you sent.

Paul continues his compliments, employing both commercial and sacrificial language. Here again it has been argued that his language was saying he needed no more from the Philippians. But we believe he was stressing their overwhelming generosity. "I have received" (ἀπέχω, *apechō*) is from a word which was normally found at the bottom of a Greek receipt. They had done all that could be expected and more. "Gifts you sent" interprets an expression (τὰ παρ' ὑμῶν, *ta par hymōn*) which is literally translated "that which was from you."

They are a fragrant offering, an acceptable sacrifice, pleasing to God.

"Fragrant offering" is an image that moves us from the accountant to the priest, and relates their gift to God. The same language is used of Christ's death in Ephesians 5:2. What they did to help Paul and his mission was also pleasing service to God (cf. Gen 8:21; Exod 29:18; Lev 1:9,13; Ezek 20:41).

The reference to Epaphroditus connects with 2:25-30, especially with verses 25 and 30.

4:19 And my God will meet all your needs

As they supplied Paul's needs, now he speaks of their needs. Some see these words as a prayer and a wish. On this view if God did not meet their needs it could be said that the prayer was simply not answered. But we believe the words have a stronger meaning. Certainly they were a prayer, but they were also a promise. God would meet their needs. But what needs were meant? In the immediate context physical needs have been at issue, though Paul's contentment indicates spiritual satisfaction as well. In the larger context of the entire letter spiritual matters are paramount, and we believe spiritual concerns cannot be left out of account here. Even if their material needs were not met, their spiritual needs would be. When would they be met? Material and spiritual needs would be met in the temporal sphere, and spiritual needs would be met at the resurrection and in the fuller fellowship with God that it would bring. In a sense this promise applies to all Christians, but we think it had special significance when expressed to friends as loyal and generous as the Philippians.

according to his glorious riches in Christ Jesus.

"Glorious riches" could describe the source of temporal blessing, with its source in God, or it could refer to the Second Coming. Cf. the other references in the book to the Second Coming (esp. the notes at 4:5). No greater source of blessing could there be (see 3:21)! "In Christ Jesus" picks up the various references to "in the Lord" found previously in the book (cf. notes at 4:1).

4:20 To our God and Father be glory for ever and ever. Amen.

The doxology catches the whole purpose of the creation. Whatever else, let God be glorified! Not that men could add to the perfection of his nature. But their lives could acknowledge and demonstrate it. So every exhortation in the book should be brought to this touchstone — "Is it to God's glory?" "Amen" is a punctuation mark, a sign of powerful assent. For this reality Paul had given all, and so should all God's people.

CONCLUSION (4:21-23)

[21]**Greet all the saints in Christ Jesus. The brothers who are with me send greetings.** [22]**All the saints send you greetings, especially those who belong to Caesar's household.** [23]**The grace of the Lord Jesus Christ be with your spirit. Amen.**

The closing greetings come from four sources: Paul, the brothers with him, all the saints, and especially those of Caesar's household. They are addressed to two groups: the primary recipients of the letter, and "all the saints." As in the opening verse of the book, the greetings take special character from being "in Christ Jesus."

Perhaps Paul wrote these closing words with his own hand, as we know he did on other occasions (1 Cor 16:21; Gal 6:11; Col 4:18; and 2 Thess 3:17). Since the letter would be read to the congregation, those called upon to greet the others may be whoever first read it. They would most likely be the "overseers and deacons." Could the greeting have been meant for some Christians outside the immediate Philippian congregation?

Neither greeters nor addressees are named. We do know the names of a number of Roman Christians from Romans 16:3-16, and some may have been in Paul's mind here. "Caesar's household" could refer to persons from high positions to lowly. They may be singled out by Paul to indicate the circles into which the gospel had penetrated. Since Philippi was a Roman colony there may have been special acquaintances between the Christians there and those of Caesar's household.

The final benediction in verse 23 is a bestowal of grace, so that the book ends as it begins (1:2).

THE BOOK OF
COLOSSIANS

INTRODUCTION

THE CITY

Colosse had been a thriving and important city several centuries before Christ, but by the time this letter was written its importance had diminished considerably, and it was overshadowed by its neighbors Hierapolis and Laodicea, both short distances to the west. Colosse was approximately 100 miles east of Ephesus, located in the Lycus valley in Asia Minor (modern Turkey). It was located on a major trade route moving inland from the coast.

A severe earthquake had shaken Laodicea either in 60 or 64 AD, and it is supposed Colosse, being near, would also have suffered. This may have been one cause of a decline in population.

The primary economic significance of the city was due to textiles, and a highly prized wool came from the area. The site of the city was rediscovered in 1835, but it has not been excavated. The city is mentioned in the New Testament only in Paul's letter.

THE CHURCH

Paul would have been in the general vicinity of Colosse during his Ephesian ministry (Acts 19) but there is no reference in Acts to a visit there, though Ephesus did become a mission center (Acts 19:10). In Colossians 1:4 Paul states that he had heard of the faith of the Colossians, and in 2:1 he speaks of those who had not met him personally. These notes, and the references to Epaphras in 1:7f and 4:12f, have led to the conclusion that Paul had not personally visited the city (though he anticipated doing so — Phlm 22), and that Epaphras was the evangelist who founded the church (1:7f). Epaphras may also have founded the congregations in Hierapolis and Laodicea (Col 4:13,16).

Several Christians from Colosse are named by Paul, including Nympha, Archippus (Col 4:15,17), Philemon, Apphia (Phlm 1f), and, of course, Epaphras. Epaphras had gone to visit Paul and is designated in Philemon 23 as Paul's "fellow prisoner" (see the notes there). The text of Colossians indicates the membership was primarily Gentiles, though the "heresy" which Paul opposed contains Jewish elements (see 2:16f and the discussion there).

OCCASION

Personal information is generally shared in letters like Colossians. This would be especially important because there would be concern over Paul's condition as a prisoner. The most likely theory is that Epaphras traveled to see Paul, primarily because of concern over certain teachings that were troubling the church and seemed to seriously diminish the significance of Christ. For some reason (imprisonment — Phlm 23?) Epaphras was unable to carry Paul's letter back to Colosse, so that task was entrusted to Tychicus, who also carried a letter to Philemon, and who was accompanied by Onesimus, a runaway slave (Col 4:7-9; Phlm 12,17).

But the troublesome teaching is the chief burden of the letter. Paul describes this heresy in 2:8,16-23, and in the rest of the book he attacks it, either frontally or in more subtle ways. The nature of the heresy has been a continuing puzzlement to scholars, and many theoretical explanations have been offered. It seems to have involved Jewish elements (2:16f), angelic worship (2:18), and extreme asceticism (2:20-23). But attempts at more precise definition have had to recognize ambiguities in the text, problems with seeing a coherent relation of the elements of the false teaching, the incompleteness of Paul's description (remembering he had to rely on the reports of others), and finding any known teaching from the period that embodied all these elements. See the discussion in the commentary proper.

The effect of this teaching was to lessen the significance of Christ's saving work. If the tenets of the heresy provided the path to salvation, then Christ's sacrifice was not as important. The heresy seems to have imported another form of works salvation, much as the circumcision party in the church attempted to do. Paul attacks the error by a powerful affirmation of Christ's identity (1:15-20) and his role in salvation. His thesis was that an understanding of Christ and life in him would completely refute the heresy. In addition to the magnificent texts in 1:15-20 and 2:9-15 he constantly makes references to benefits which the heretics sought after, but which only Christ truly gave. These included such things as wisdom, knowledge, and fullness (cf. 1:9). Note also the references to the mystery (1:26; 2:2). Even the ethical appeals from 3:1–4:6 powerfully emphasize the relation of the ethical life to Christ (note the references listed before 3:1).

PAUL'S LOCALE

The commonly accepted tradition holds that Paul wrote Colossians and Philemon from the Roman imprisonment described in Acts 28. The apostle does not name the city from which he writes, but numerous factors support Rome. Luke (Col 4:14) and Aristarchus (Colossians 4:10) were with him there, and were in Rome according to Acts 27:2 (the "we" implies Luke). Acts indicates Paul's Roman imprisonment was not unduly restrictive (Acts 28:30f) and this fits the relatively unfettered activities described in Colossians 4:7-15. Onesimus was with Paul (Col 4:9; cf. Phlm) and it is quite possible he had migrated to Rome to lose himself in the urban populace. If we accept the Roman hypothesis, Colossians would be dated in the early 60s.

Due to the perceived presence of problems with a Roman origin, however, other locales have been suggested. One is Caesarea, since that is the only other Pauline imprisonment documented in Acts. This theory has not gained any significant following, since the circumstances described in Acts do not fit those depicted in Colossians and Philemon, especially Paul's expectation to visit Colosse (Phlm 22). From Caesarea Paul expected only to go to Rome, and before his appeal to Caesar he was kept in continual uncertainty.

A more likely case has been formed for Ephesus. It was relatively close to Colosse and could thus conveniently explain Paul's travel plans (i.e., an eventual trip to Rome after a detour to Colosse). Paul did encounter some problems in Ephesus (1 Cor 4:9-13; 2 Cor 4:8-12; 6:4f; 11:23-25; and perhaps 1 Cor 15:32). They might have included prison, but Acts gives no evidence of it, and details are uncertain enough to disallow any definite conclusion. Since Luke details Paul's problems so carefully, it seems strange he would not mention an Ephesian imprisonment had there been one. Further, Acts has no indication Luke was even in Ephesus. He was left in Philippi on Paul's second tour, and did not resume the apostle's company till the third tour (Acts 16:16,40; 20:5). If Colossians was written from Ephesus, it would be dated in the early to mid 50s.

The case for Ephesus depends, in part, on certain perceived weaknesses in the Roman view. One is the divergence between Paul's announced intent to go to Spain (Rom 15:28) and his desire to return to Colosse (Phlm 22). In our comments on Philemon 22 we have argued that a change of plans by Paul is a reasonable supposition. Another objection is the distance from Rome to Colosse, well over 1000 miles. If Paul expected Onesimus to be returned to him (see notes on Philemon) that seems a long distance for him to be sent only to retrace his steps. However, the Roman road system was good, and Paul's honor demanded that he send Onesimus and give Philemon the option of voluntary response, whatever the distance. We do not think Paul could have written as he did to Philemon and not have sent Onesimus.

A third argument has to do with Paul's request for lodging with Philemon (v. 22). Would he have made such a request when so many miles and days away? But once we accept Paul's intent to visit Colosse (perhaps to deal with the heresy) and consider his graciousness in dealing with Philemon, the request seems reasonable enough.

A fair case can be made for Ephesus, but we hold that the case for Rome is the stronger alternative.

OUTLINE

A. Tychicus and Onesimus — 4:7-9
B. Greetings — 4:10-15
C. Concluding Instructions — 4:16-18

BIBLIOGRAPHY
COLOSSIANS

Bruce, F.F. *The Epistles to the Colossians, to Philemon, and to the Ephesians*. Grand Rapids: Eerdmans, 1984.

Lohse, Eduard. *Colossians and Philemon*. Philadelphia: Fortress, 1971.

Melick, Richard. *Philippians, Colossians, Philemon*. Nashville: Broadman, 1991.

O'Brien, Peter. *Colossians, Philemon*. Waco: Word Books, 1982.

Patzia, Arthur. *Ephesians, Colossians, Philemon*. Peabody, MA: Hendrickson, 1984.

Pokorný, Petr. *Colossians, A Commentary*. Peabody, MA: Hendrickson, 1991.

Weed, Michael. *The Letters of Paul to the Ephesians, Colossians, and Philemon*. Austin: Sweet, 1971.

COLOSSIANS 1

SALUTATION (1:1-2)

¹Paul, an apostle of Christ Jesus by the will of God, and Timothy our brother,

²To the holy and faithful[a] brothers in Christ at Colosse: Grace and peace to you from God our Father.[b]

[a]2 Or *believing*   [b]2 Some manuscripts *Father and the Lord Jesus Christ*

1:1 Paul, an apostle of Christ Jesus by the will of God,

The epistle opens in the usual form for letters of the day. To most Colossian Christians Paul was just a name, since he had never been there personally. In all his letters except Philippians, Philemon, and 1 and 2 Thessalonians he introduced himself as an "apostle." This was probably done for various reasons, and here it may have been to give weight to his words for a church he had never visited. The impression was enhanced by his indication of the source of his call ("of Jesus Christ by the will of God"). Such a person's words could not be taken lightly.

and Timothy our brother,

Timothy's name was joined to Paul's in 1 and 2 Thessalonians, 2 Corinthians, Philippians and Philemon. Colossians 4:18 indicates he was not a coauthor of the letter. Of all Paul's companions "in chains" (4:7-14) Timothy may have been singled out because of a special relation to Paul as a permanent coworker. We do not know what previous relations, if any, he had with the Colossian church, though we can suppose he was

145

known to them by name. Was inclusion of his name a second-person verification of Paul's message, or was it to mark Timothy as a preacher of the true gospel? Or was there some other reason?

1:2 To the holy and faithful

The word for "holy" (ἅγιοι, *hagioi*) or a cognate is the term of greeting in all of Paul's letters to churches except 1 and 2 Thessalonians and Galatians. It indicates that they had been chosen and set apart by God — a special people. In some contexts the term indicates a holy lifestyle, but that would be a strange meaning in greeting a church like Corinth. Thus "saints" (the noun form) is the preferred meaning, and even with "holy" as in the NIV, it is God's choice, not their conduct, which is to be understood.

"Faithful" (πιστοί, *pistoi*) could mean "believers" in contrast to the outsiders who did not believe in Christ. But that meaning could be indicated simply by saying "in Christ." Therefore we prefer to see "faithful" as meaning "steadfast." Thus it would be an early encouragement to be true to Christ in the face of heresy.

brothers in Christ at Colosse:

"In Christ" or a similar expression punctuates the book at many points (1:4,14,16,17,19; 2:3,9,10,11,12,15 [in Greek]; 3:18,20 [Greek]; 4:7 and 17). It meant "as Christians" and the frequency of such references here as elsewhere indicated the all-encompassing scope of the new life.

Grace and peace to you

The greeting "grace and peace" was a Christian application of the form of secular letters (see the comments on Phil 1:2). Given the nature of Christian interrelationships, it would indicate a deep and prayerful concern for one another, rather than a perfunctory greeting. Among the blessings made possible by divine grace was "peace" (εἰρήνη, *eirēnē*, "well-being"). On peace see 1:15 and 3:20. The salutation thus combines

Greek and Hebrew greetings in a Christian context and wishes an enhancement of blessings already received. "From God" says that they were not generated just from man, but were divinely granted. The highest power in the universe was called upon in these simple words. Grace surrounds the letter, being found again in 4:18.

from God our Father.

Normally Pauline greetings were from God and from "the Lord Jesus Christ." Though the reference to Christ is absent here, the body of the letter will present Christ to readers in an unforgettable way.

I. THANKSGIVING (1:3-8)

[3]We always thank God, the Father of our Lord Jesus Christ, when we pray for you, [4]because we have heard of your faith in Christ Jesus and of the love you have for all the saints — [5]the faith and love that spring from the hope that is stored up for you in heaven and that you have already heard about in the word of truth, the gospel [6]that has come to you. All over the world this gospel is bearing fruit and growing, just as it has been doing among you since the day you heard it and understood God's grace in all its truth. [7]You learned it from Epaphras, our dear fellow servant, who is a faithful minister of Christ on our[a] behalf, [8]and who also told us of your love in the Spirit.

[a]7 Some manuscripts *your*

These verses thank God for his grace given to the Colossians as well as given all over the world. Verses 3 through 8 are one sentence in Greek, and it is at times difficult to interpret exactly. The Hellenistic letter form is followed, but it is given a distinctly Christian stamp. Following this paragraph is Paul's prayer, based upon what is described in the present verses. Paul speaks of the Colossians in verses 3-6a, then of the worldwide influence of the gospel in 6b. In the remainder of verse 6 and in verse 7 he returns to consider the Colossians. The progress of their faith was from preaching (by Epaphras, v. 7) to hope (v. 5) to love (v. 4) to Paul's prayers (vv. 8ff).

1:3 We always thank God, the Father of our Lord Jesus Christ, when we pray for you,

Jesus is first mentioned in this verse. He is introduced as "Lord" (κύριος, *kyrios*), and his Lordship is constantly on display throughout the epistle. It draws powerful significance from the hymn in 1:15-20. We are invited by the ways this book will describe Jesus to make comparison with the way he is presented in the first three gospels. Such a comparison helps us appreciate how God had enlarged the church's perception of the one who was "Lord and Christ."

"Thanks" to God is a conspicuous note in Colossians (cf. 1:12; 2:7; 3:15,16,17; 4:2). Here it was a plural thanksgiving, indicating Timothy, and likely others, joined Paul in prayer. Perhaps regular group prayers by those in Paul's company are implied. "Always" implies a constancy in the prayers, as well as a continuing gratitude. God was called "Father" in a scattering of Old Testament references, but fatherhood here is because of Christ, his Son, and because Christians are God's sons in a special way. In other words, God is seen differently because of Jesus.

The content of the prayer will be given in verses 9-12. See also 4:2-4,12.

1:4 because we have heard of your faith in Christ Jesus

Now the reason for the thanks is given. It was due to their faith and love response to the hope given by God. Faith, hope, and love are often grouped in Paul's writings (1 Cor 13:13; Rom 5:1-5; Gal 5:5f; 1 Thess 3:5-8) and one or more, as here, is often the reason for his thanksgiving. Reference to their love recurs in verse 8.

Two views are held of the expression "in Christ Jesus." One maintains that it was trust in Christ as the way of salvation. The other, which most commentators prefer, sees it as the sphere in which Christians lived. Thus those "in Christ Jesus" were the people who lived by faith. This makes "in Christ Jesus" parallel with "all the saints." This preferable view still leads one to ask "faith in what or whom," and the answer must have included, but was not limited to, the first view.

and of the love you have for all the saints —

Though Jesus called upon his followers to exercise universal love (Luke 6:27ff) here the special love within the believing community is noted.

1:5 the faith and love that spring from the hope that is stored up for you in heaven

"The faith and the love" of the NIV are repeated for clarity, though the expression is not in the Greek. As the NIV renders it, faith and love spring from hope. This is the most likely meaning, though some suggest it was the prayer (v. 3) that sprang from awareness of their hope. Perhaps the ultimate difference in the views is slight. Hope is referred to again in verse 23, as a sustaining foundation. Since Paul's primary concern in this letter was the heresy (2:8-23) he may have been implying that the false teaching robbed them of the hope Jesus gave them, or that it made the achieving of hope more difficult through its requirements. If they had hope as Christians, what more could the heresy offer? Of course uncertainty about the exact nature of the heresy makes this only a conjecture. Though hope has to do with the future, it also influences the present.

"Stored up in heaven" indicates the origin of hope, as well as the sureness of it. It is safe beyond man's meddling and thus assures ultimate glory (1:27; 3:4).

and that you have already heard about in the word of truth, the gospel

The hope-giving message, the "word of truth," had been basic to their calling from the beginning (v. 6a), unlike any "johnny-come-lately" philosophy (2:8). "Truth" (ἀλήθεια, *alētheia*) is found both here and in the next verse. The Hebrew sense of the word was "reliability." The Greek sense indicated the true in contrast to the false. Perhaps both ideas are implied here. Truth could be depended upon to give hope, and it dealt the death knell to false teaching (as Paul would go on to show).

1:6 that has come to you. All over the world this gospel is bearing fruit and growing,

A more appropriate verse division would include the first five words of verse 6 (four words in Greek) with verse 5. The gospel is universal, and powerfully produces fruit and grows. These qualities contrasted with the heresy, and marked the heresy for what it was — something other than the true gospel (assuming the false teaching presented itself as Christian.) It did not bear the appropriate marks.

just as it has been doing among you since the day you heard it and understood God's grace in all its truth.

Though the gospel was preached by men like Epaphras and Paul, the stress was on the power of God's message ("an internal energy," says one author), beyond the realm of human effort. This power resulted in multiplication of converts as well as in transforming lives more and more into the likeness of Christ. Paul prayed for this growth to happen in the experience of the Colossians in verse 10.

"Grace" picks up the greeting of verse 2, and "in truth" restates the language of verse 5.

1:7 You learned it from Epaphras, our dear fellow servant, who is a faithful minister of Christ on our behalf,

"Learned" (from μανθάνω, *manthanō*) is not the term Paul normally used for communication or reception of the gospel. Perhaps the term had significance in contrast to the false teaching. Epaphras is mentioned also in 4:12f and Philemon 23 (called a "fellow prisoner for Christ Jesus"). He planted the gospel in Colosse. Paul's reference to him authenticated the

message he brought as "the word of truth of the gospel" —
again against heresy, and also complimented him generously.
The Greek term translated "fellow servant" (σύνδουλος, *syn-
doulos*) is found elsewhere only in 4:7 (of Tychicus). If "our"
behalf is read this fits Paul's endorsement of Epaphras. He did
his work as Paul's emissary. However, some translators prefer
"your" (NIV footnote) and the Greek would allow either reading. "Your" would fit verse 8, which indicates Epaphras was
sent from Colosse to Paul with news of the church.

1:8 and who also told us of your love in the Spirit.

This verse testifies to the universality of the love Christians
practiced. They had never met Paul, but loved him. This may
have been partly because they knew Paul had sent Epaphras
their way in the beginning. It may also imply more communication between Paul and this church than the New Testament
reveals.

This verse has the only reference to the Spirit in the book
(though see 2:5). It speaks to God's working within them to
create a loving lifestyle.

II. PAUL'S PRAYER FOR THE COLOSSIANS (1:9-14)

[9]**For this reason, since the day we heard about you, we
have not stopped praying for you and asking God to fill you
with the knowledge of his will through all spiritual wisdom
and understanding. [10]And we pray this in order that you may
live a life worthy of the Lord and may please him in every
way: bearing fruit in every good work, growing in the knowledge of God, [11]being strengthened with all power according
to his glorious might so that you may have great endurance
and patience, and joyfully [12]giving thanks to the Father, who
has qualified you[a] to share in the inheritance of the saints in
the kingdom of light. [13]For he has rescued us from the
dominion of darkness and brought us into the kingdom of**

**the Son he loves, [14]in whom we have redemption,[b] the for-
giveness of sins.**

[a]*12* **Some manuscripts** *us*   [b]*14* **A few late manuscripts** *redemption
through his blood*

The prayer, beginning here, is consequent upon what has
been said in verses three through eight. There is disagreement
over the structure of this section. Some see the prayer as
extending through verse 12, but with an exposition of 12 in
the next two verses. Others have the prayer ending in verse 11,
with verses 12-14 being drawn from a baptismal confession of
the church. Verses 12-14, then, would introduce the Christ
hymn of verses 15-20. Verses 12-14 certainly seem to be baptismal language, and the importance of baptism is pivotal to
Paul's development of the idea of what it meant to be in Christ
(2:11f). The way the text is analyzed, however, does not signif-
icantly alter the meaning of it.

There are numerous correspondences between this paragraph and the thanksgiving in verses 3 through 8. This follows
Paul's usual procedure of praying for what he had noted in his
thanksgiving. O'Brien lists the following: "since the day" (vv. 6,
9), "we heard" (vv. 4,9), "knowledge" (vv. 4,9,10), "bearing fruit
and increasing" (vv. 6,10), "giving thanks" (vv. 3,12), "the Father"
(vv. 3,12), "the saints" (vv. 4, 12), "Spirit/in spirit" (vv. 8,9),
"hope/inheritance" (vv. 5,12), and "all" (vv. 4,6, 9,10,11).[1]

1:9 For this reason, since the day we heard about you, we have not stopped praying for you

Prayers of intercession can vary in motivation and in content.
Paul's special prayers here fit the Colossian situation. They were
not just "prayer in general." The motivation/reason of this
prayer was stated in verses 3-5. The "day we heard" may indicate
particular information about the Colossian church, perhaps
even about the intrusion of the heresy. Or it may indicate all the
time since the very first report to Paul about the church. In the

---

[1]Peter O'Brien, *Colossians, Philemon* (Waco: Word Books, 1982), p. 18.

latter case the verse testifies to the persistence and depth of Paul's concern, even for those he had not met personally.

and asking God to fill you with the knowledge of his will

Three terms indicate the burden of the prayer. The word for "knowledge" (ἐπίγνωσις, *epignōsis*) used here (also in 2:2; 3:10) is not the usual Greek γνῶσις (*gnōsis*). The Greek term for "wisdom" (σοφία, *sophia*) is also in 1:28; 2:3; 3:16 and 4:5; and that for "understanding" (σύνεσις, *synesis*) recurs in 2:2. These three terms were significant against the claims of the heresy, with its "hollow and deceptive philosophies" (2:8).

Paul prayed they would be filled with "knowledge." The filling idea is used often in Colossians (1:19,24,25; 2:2,3,9,10; 4:12,17) and likely confuted any claims by the false teachers to offer fullness. "Knowledge," "wisdom" and "understanding" would lead to proper living (v. 10). The process would be empowered by God (v. 11). But exactly what was this knowledge "of his will"? The basic truths of Christianity were already at their disposal. Likely what was involved was a deeper understanding which would enhance obedience to God (cf. "growing in knowledge" in v. 10), fruit bearing, and the insight to discern how the heresy was destructive of God's work in Christ. Such a prayer is appropriate for all Christians in every age, since none has completely grasped the complete significance of what Christ has done and how men may respond to it.

through all spiritual wisdom and understanding.

We are not told how this knowledge would be given. It would involve God's power. It would be spiritual (some see the Spirit's work here). There were many ways God could work to accomplish these ends. They could include interaction, meditation, divinely guided insight, instruction and worship.

1:10 And we pray this in order that you may live a life worthy of the Lord and may please him in every way:

"And we pray this" is added by the NIV translators for clarity, as is "him" in midverse. To know was to obey, and

knowledge was the instrument to obedience, as obedience fur-
thered knowledge. Being Christian builds on itself, through
God's power (v. 11). Clearly there is no division here between
mental grasp and Christian action. The two work in tandem,
strengthening one another.

bearing fruit in every good work, growing in the knowledge of God,

Paul used four participles to carry his petition for their spiritual growth. They are the words translated "bearing," "growing," "being strengthened" (v. 11), and "giving thanks" (v. 12).
Because verse 12 continues the participial construction some
scholars are reluctant to see a separate baptismal confession
beginning at this point (see the discussion preceding v. 9).
These four explain the "worthy" and pleasing life. The first two
terms described the progress of the gospel in verse 6.

1:11 being strengthened with all power according to his glorious might

Prayer implies divine action. Paul did not just exhort the
Colossians to try harder. He assured them resources would be
more than adequate for their needs. Who could doubt that the
heresy would be successfully encountered when confronted by
God's "glorious might"? "Glorious" (δόξα, *doxa*) gives a quali-
tative dimension that goes beyond force or energy (cf. the
term in 1:29). The term κράτος (*kratos*), translated "might,"
never refers to merely human power in the New Testament.

so that you may have great endurance and patience, and joyfully

"Endurance," "patience" and "joy," when inspired by God's
power, would be more than passive qualities. Endurance was
the quality that would hold against enemy assaults in battle, or
that would persevere in a race (cf. Heb 12:1; Luke 8:15). It
would stand against heretical pressure. Patience was a fruit of
the Spirit (Gal 5:22; and see Col 3:12). The term basically
denoted relations to one's fellow.

NIV connects "joyfully" with "thanksgiving" (v. 12), but others maintain it could modify "endurance" and "patience." The Stoics admired patience, but it was the Christians who combined patience with joy.

1:12 giving thanks to the Father,

Though "giving thanks" is the last of the four participles in verses 10-12 (see discussion at v. 10) the act could be seen as a human response to the divine empowering of verses 10 and 11. Lohse argues that Paul never closed his intercessions with thanks, and thus this was a new beginning. There are parallels in verses 12-14 to baptismal language. Deliverance from death and forgiveness parallel 2:12f (similar concepts are found in 1 Cor 1:30 and 1 Pet 1:3-5). Thus these verses could reflect baptismal language employed in the early church. If so, the brothers were called to reflect on their conversions and the great gratitude generated by what God had done for them. There may be no higher and more powerful motivation for submission to the Lord than gratitude for his grace.

who has qualified you to share in the inheritance of the saints

The "inheritance" (κλῆρος, *klēros*) draws from the Old Testament background of Israel's possession of Canaan. The word recurs in 3:24. The "blessing" here is present, but a present with a future. There are two views of "saints," or "holy ones." One holds them to be fellow believers, as in other usages in Colossians as well as in Acts 20:32 and 26:18. The other considers them to be angels, on the basis of parallels at Qumran (cf. Dan 7:18,22). This position argues that such fellowship is set against the heretical "worship of angels" in 2:18. Linguistically and theologically either is possible, though we do not know which Paul had in mind. We consider the former more likely.

in the kingdom of light.

"Kingdom of light" and "dominion of darkness" (v. 13) reflect a theme often employed in Scripture for the contrast of good and evil (see Acts 26:18). It was found both in Hellenistic Judaism and at Qumran.

1:13 For he has rescued us from the dominion of darkness and brought us into the kingdom of the Son he loves,

Paul now includes himself among the "rescued" (contrast "you" in v. 12 with "us" here). "Rescued" and "brought" imply an act of transfer. If this was baptismal language then baptism was that act. God had moved a population from danger to safety, from Satan's dominion to Christ's. "Kingdom" is repeated from verse 12, but here it is not the usual "kingdom of God" but "kingdom of his Son." Paul refers to Christ's present rule, before that time when the kingdom would be delivered up to the Father (1 Cor 15:23-28). "Kingdom of the Son" also prepares for the depiction of Christ to follow in verses 15-20.

1:14 in whom we have redemption, the forgiveness of sins.

The transition involved deliverance from sin. The expression "forgiveness of sins," though often in Acts, is in Paul only here and in Ephesians 1:7. The emphasis here may have related to some claim of the heretics to offer forgiveness, though we have no direct evidence on the point.

III. THE HYMN ABOUT CHRIST (1:15-20)

[15]**He is the image of the invisible God, the firstborn over all creation.** [16]**For by him all things were created: things in heaven and on earth, visible and invisible, whether thrones or powers or rulers or authorities; all things were created by him and for him.** [17]**He is before all things, and in him all things hold together.** [18]**And he is the head of the body, the church; he is the beginning and the firstborn from among the dead, so that in everything he might have the supremacy.** [19]**For God was pleased to have all his fullness dwell in him,** [20]**and through him to reconcile to himself all things, whether**

things on earth or things in heaven, by making peace through his blood, shed on the cross.

These magnificent words form the heart of Paul's presentation of Christ in Colossians, and it is from this base that he attacked the heresy described in chapter 2. Had one known the human Jesus personally, one could hardly have imagined the truths about him expressed here. But when Jesus was raised from the dead, Christian understanding broadened and deepened, as the wonder of God's action became known in increasingly greater glory.

These verses are stylistically different from the first person "confession" which preceded in verses 12-14, and from the direct application style of the following verses (1:21ff). Because of style and language there is general agreement that verses 15-20 were a hymn, though we must recognize the ancient and modern definitions of that term are not identical. Even in English translation one can sense the rhythm and symmetry of these words.

When and where, then, did the hymn originate? Was it in a context outside Christianity, then taken and adapted by Christians? Those holding this view have suggested both Greek and Jewish (Hellenistic and rabbinic) origins, but no scholarly consensus has arisen. Was it originally Christian, drawing on concepts which were in the surrounding world, but were not in hymnic form? In any of these cases, did Paul take available material and rework it for his purposes? If so, and if one could determine the points in the hymn at which Paul edited and revised, that would be helpful in determining the ideas he was combatting. Numerous suggestions have been made regarding any Pauline revisions, but again there is no consensus.

Those convinced that an earlier hymn received Christian adaptation have conjectured how the original might have been structured. By theorizing what additions or changes were made various original strophic arrangements have been suggested. Some of the possible changes can be seen in the following discussion. Whatever its original form, the hymn as it stands first describes Christ and the cosmos (vv. 15-17) and then Christ and the church (vv. 18-20). Parallels can be seen within the two parts of the hymn. For example both parts describe him as "first-born" (vv. 15,18), and in each case the following clause has the same Greek construction. "Thrones . . . authorities" in verse 16 parallels "things . . . heaven" in verse 20.

A minority of scholars consider the hymn to be entirely Paul's composition. Though perhaps not an insurmountable argument, critics of this view point out that the language of the hymn differs from Paul's other writings both in vocabulary and in form. Pauline authorship could still allow his use of materials and concepts from the surrounding thought world. And if Paul were the author, had he composed this hymn on some other occasion and modified it here, or was it composed just for this letter? And if just for this letter, why did he employ the apparent hymn form? Would he intend that his depiction of Christ in refutation of the heresy would be given greater force by working it into Christian worship? The hymn form would certainly be more memorable. Paul's effective use of the hymn indicates the heretics would also know of it, and that the church would understand the concepts set forth in it.

1:15 He is the image of the invisible God,

These are amazing assertions about one whom the Romans had executed as a troublemaker short decades before. Jesus is first called the image of the invisible God (cf. 2 Cor 4:4). He revealed God's nature and will to man, making the unseen seen, the unknown known, the known revealed with greater clarity. Why was the term "image" (εἰκών, *eikōn*) used? A possible source was the story of the creation of man in God's image (Gen 1:27), with the implication that Jesus was what Adam, because of the fall, failed to be. But elsewhere the hymn uses language associated with the wisdom tradition in Israel. Wisdom 7:25 depicts wisdom, personified, as being the "image" (*eikōn*) of God. Proverbs 8:22 speaks of wisdom being with God at the beginning of creation. Some Jewish traditions also associate "in the beginning" of Gen 1:1 with wisdom. So if the image was wisdom, and "firstborn" indicated creation, the idea would be that by wisdom God created. Thus Paul may have borrowed from these ideas to give substance to the word "image" used of Jesus. He revealed God's wisdom, his will, to man. He was also the Creator, thus existed from the beginning. The "image" concept may have drawn its meaning from one of the backgrounds indicated, but this does not exhaust the implications of the language for the reflective believer. Jesus was the one who possessed God's authority among men. He made possible a kind of access to God previously unknown. These words set the Christ in a position from which no heresy dare unseat him.

the firstborn over all creation.

Next Jesus is designated "the firstborn" (πρωτότοκος, *prōto-tokos*) over all creation. Any suspicion that this would imply Jesus was part of creation is dispelled as the text continues into verse 16, which twice speaks of his creation of "all things," and verse 17 with "he is before all things." Here Paul pictured him as unique beyond the creation. The Old Testament twice (Exod 4:22, Jer 31:9) uses "firstborn" to describe one specially loved by the Father. Here the idea also stresses his supremacy over creation, especially as developed in subsequent verses. Cf. also Heb 1:6 where the word "firstborn" is a Messianic title.

1:16 For by him all things were created: things in heaven and on earth, visible and invisible, whether thrones or powers or rulers or authorities;

The meaning of "firstborn" is fleshed out in this and the following verse. The first reference to creation indicates completed action in the past (aorist), while the second reference (perfect) stresses the continuance of the creation's existence. "By him" is literally "in him," and some translations so render the Greek. Some see Christ as the instrument of creation, as in John 1:3; 1 Corinthians 8:6; and on the basis of the Jewish wisdom tradition. Others see "in him" as the location or sphere of creation, as in Ephesians 1:4. Some argue both meanings may have been intended. How nuanced did Paul intend to be in his use of prepositions?

"All things" are defined by the rest of the verse. Since all have one creator, all that exists has a unity. It was cosmos, not chaos. Things in heaven, on earth, visible and invisible, include thrones, powers, rulers and authorities. In Jewish thought thrones and power often indicated angelic hosts (2 Enoch 20:1; Test Levi 3:8). Rulers and authorities are referred to in Romans 8:38; 1 Corinthians 15:24; Ephesians 1:21 and 6:12. These are generally held to be spiritual powers as well. The New Testament, however, does not give enough data to depict a hierarchy of such powers. Whether good or evil, all were his creations. Paul does not discuss the problem of God creating evil powers. It is usual to affirm God made them free and they chose evil. Scholars differ regarding whether any moral implications regarding the "thrones," etc., are even intended here. Quite likely there was reference here to some aspect of the heresy, so that the supremacy of Christ over any role given to any of them is clear.

all things were created by him and for him.

The absoluteness of the creative power is enforced by the twofold repetition of "all things." The verse ends by repeating the creative refrain, but now as "by him and for him." Here different prepositions were used from the opening statement of the verse. "By (through) him" clearly shows him as the creative agent. He was both originator and goal (further stressed in v. 17) of all creation. Any movement in history in any other direction was in the wrong direction. So was any system that sought to move beyond or escape history.

1:17 He is before all things, and in him all things hold together.

"Before" introduces a fourth Greek pronoun (πρό, *pro*), with "by" (ἐν, *en*), "by" (διά, *dia*), and "for" (εἰς, *eis*, "into/unto") of verse 16. "Before" probably picks up the sense of "firstborn" of verse 15. The prevailing idea seems to indicate his priority over all things. "Hold together" (συνίστημι, *synistēmi*) is implied by his creative activity. Jesus is the "glue" of all that exists. The Greek term means to continue or endure. Without him there would be chaos, dissolution, disintegration (cf. a similar role for wisdom in Wisd Sol 1:4; 7:24). Consider how this concept would impact any teaching which minimized the significance and role of Christ. Note how later exhortation constantly refers back to Christ (3:10,13,15,16,17,18,24).

1:18 And he is the head of the body, the church;

We have already noted scholarly disagreement over the division of this hymn into sections. One view considers 15f as describing the creative Christ, and 17-18a as depicting him as Lord of the universe and head of the church. Then the rest of the passage stresses his role as reconciler. Other discussion has centered on "the church." It has been argued that "body" (σῶμα, *sōma*) in Hellenistic thought could refer to the cosmos. Thus, the position states, the hymn originally continued its cosmic significance through the term "body," and the reference to "beginning and firstborn," parallel to verse 15, begins the second section of the hymn. Paul, on this view, added "the church," thus giving a different meaning to "body," and changing the thrust of verse 17. Of course all these theories are only conjectural. An objection to this view is that Paul never used "body" in the Hellenistic sense. On the other hand it would be a powerful statement of the importance of the church for a term which had indicated the cosmos to now indicate Christ's followers.

It can be asked why Paul chose the body image to describe the church. It may come from the Old Testament concept of the unity of the people of God, "corporate personality," in which the entire community was seen as a single entity and suffered or was blessed because of the actions of one part (cf. Achan in Josh 7), usually a leader. It is possible the idea became significant when the Lord told Paul on the Damascus road that to persecute Jesus' people was to persecute Jesus himself (Acts 9:5).

The body image was also used by Paul in Romans 12:4f; 1 Corinthians 12:12-26; Ephesians 4:15f, 5:23, and later in Colossians 2:9 and 3:15. It stresses the organic connection of Christ and his people, beyond the connection already implied by creation and sustaining power. It indicates the special place of the church to the Creator of the cosmos. "Thrones . . . authorities" are not called his body. As Bruce observes, we think of the head as vitalizing and energizing the church and using it as the instrument for his work on earth.[2] As the church preached Christ, his Lordship over the cosmos was forthtold as well. The high significance thus given the church may have been to counter an individualistic tendency in the "heresy."

he is the beginning and the firstborn from among the dead,

"Beginning" (αρχή, *archē*) and "firstborn" here refer to the "creation" of the church through Christ's resurrection. Since he was firstborn he made it possible for others to be "born from the dead." "Firstborn" may mean he was the first victor over death, but it may indicate his authority (as it did in v. 15) over death as it was over all creation. He produced and ruled both the old and the new creation. The "and" between "beginning" and "firstborn" is not in the Greek, so that "firstborn" modifies "beginning" rather than being a separate description.

so that in everything he might have the supremacy.

"Everything" catches the universal language ("all" in 15, 16 twice, 17 twice, 19 and 20) found throughout this paragraph. "Supremacy" (the verb πρωτεύω, *prōteuō*, "to be first") underlines the point already made. The following two verses will give further substance to Christ's relation to his body.

1:19 For God was pleased to have all his fullness dwell in him,

"God" is not found in the Greek, so the verse could be translated with "fullness" (πλήρωμα, *plērōma*) as the subject

---

[2]F.F. Bruce, *The Epistles to the Colossians, to Philemon, and to the Ephesians* (Grand Rapids: Eerdmans, 1984), p. 68.

("all fullness was pleased to dwell in him"), or a subject could be supplied, which would be "God." In context both translations say the same thing about Christ (cf. 2:9). The reference to "fullness" may be aimed at some claim of the heresy, perhaps that some (intermediate between God and man) beings other than Christ possessed God's fullness. Though the concept has depths we cannot fathom, here it should probably be understood as indicating the role of Christ described in this paragraph. In him God's attributes and activities, directed toward reconciliation, were found. Nothing necessary for that to occur was missing. And if the fullness was in Christ, why accept any system of thought ("philosophy" — 2:8) that indicated otherwise?

1:20 and through him to reconcile to himself all things, whether things on earth or things in heaven,

When the central theme of salvation and reconciliation is at last broached, it comes with the greatest of all introductions, set into a background of absolute power and majesty (vv. 15-19). It is in reconciliation that human concerns touch divine action. But Paul's view of reconciliation was broader than peace between man and God. It sweeps through earth and heaven and encompasses all of reality. Some maintain that the heresy posited an inherent conflict between God and the creation. Paul denied it. He saw all discord in humanity and nature resolved through Christ. The chaos brought on by the fall was overcome. What had gone wrong God then made right. Enmity was replaced by love.

All this was made possible but was actualized only in part — primarily in the redeemed community. The powers still had their day and could oppose God. But they were not sovereign. Implied here is a safety in Christ from such forces. Whether the powers, human or transhuman, that continue to resist God would one day be compelled to submission is a topic Paul does not address here. But the picture painted of Christ leaves no doubt as to what this outcome would be.

by making peace through his blood, shed on the cross.

If ever there was a shocking contrast, the last of this verse
affords it. Having been carried to cosmic heights and having
contemplated the very originating and sustaining power of the
universe, we are now transported to the dismal scene of crucifixion and shed blood. Yet that was how God, the "master of
surprises," had made reconciliation possible (cf. Phil 2:5-11).
Could this scene of victory through humiliation have any application to heretical pride?

IV. THE HYMN APPLIED (1:21-23)

[21]**Once you were alienated from God and were enemies in
your minds because of**[a] **your evil behavior.** [22]**But now he has
reconciled you by Christ's physical body through death to
present you holy in his sight, without blemish and free from
accusation —** [23]**if you continue in your faith, established and
firm, not moved from the hope held out in the gospel. This
is the gospel that you heard and that has been proclaimed to
every creature under heaven, and of which I, Paul, have
become a servant.**

[a]*21 Or minds as shown by*

The style of writing changes abruptly here as Paul applies the
truths he has just depicted to his readers. One author has called
it a homiletic adaptation of the hymn. (Of what use is theology if
it does not impact human existence?) The NIV supplies "from
God." The theme of reconciliation, resumed from verse 20, is
first discussed from the negative side (alienation). In his extensive depiction of their status in Christ here and in 2:9-15 Paul
indicates the utter folly of turning from Christ. Verse 23 is an
exhortation to insure it would not happen. The point is reinforced by the "once" and "now" of verses 21 and 22.

**1:21 Once you were alienated from God and were enemies in
your minds because of your evil behavior.**

The language here applies, in a sense, to all men. But in this letter the application was primarily to Gentiles (cf. 3:7) who had never been in covenant with God. Now the alienation implied in verse 20 is made specific. It consisted of thoughts and deeds (behavior). On "minds" (διάνοια, *dianoia*) cf. Ephesians 2:3 and 4:18. This was the way of the "dominion of darkness" (v. 13). The reference to their evil prepares us for the next verse, and for the paranetic materials in chapters 3 and 4.

"From God," not in the Greek, is added in the NIV for clarity.

1:22 But now he has reconciled you by Christ's physical body through death

The first half of this verse repeats the thought of verse 20. The last half echoes the prayer of 1:10. "Reconciled" is picked up from verse 20, and "all things" of that verse is drawn into narrower focus on the Colossians. The reference to Christ's physical body distinguishes it from the church as his body. Man, God's enemy, could not heal the rupture with his Creator. No effort, no matter how great, would avail. Only Christ's death could abolish the hostility.

to present you holy in his sight, without blemish and free from accusation —

The goal in practice was holiness, freedom from blemish and freedom from accusation. Some consider this language to be drawn from sacrificial terminology, though the fit is not exact. Others consider it judicial, as if one were presented blameless in court. The blessed consequence was the same, whether Paul had in mind one or neither of these images.

When was the presenting to be done? At the second coming? Certainly that. But a person is also so presented in this life, through the reconciling blood. There could be no such presentation at the second coming if the reality were not operating in the present. Verse 23 speaks of continuing in the faith. This would be done, in part, by maintaining the proper conduct.

"Holy" (ἅγιοι, *hagioi*) basically means "set apart" and is the same word as "saints" (1:4). The context here, however, seems also to imply the meaning of holiness which indicates purity of life — the usual meaning given today.

1:23 if you continue in your faith, established and firm, not moved from the hope held out in the gospel.

Christ's death was the divine act, but the resultant holiness and life quality was both a divine gift and a human responsibility. The NIV translates "your" faith, indicating personal faith. Other translations, in accord with the Greek, translate "the faith," which could mean the Christian teaching handed down. The result in life is the same in either case. On faith and hope see 1:5. "Established" (from θεμελιόω, *themelioō*) and "firm" (ἑδραῖοι, *hedraioi*) use building imagery and employ the same terminology used in describing building on the rock in Matthew 7:24f. See also Ephesians 2:20. "Hope" prepares us for 1:27, and implies that movement to a heretical position could destroy that hope.

This is the gospel that you heard and that has been proclaimed to every creature under heaven,

The NIV also adds "This is the gospel," repeating for clearer sentence structure. "Every creature under heaven" is obviously not to be taken literally. Paul's point was that the message they accepted was the same one offered wherever Christianity had gone. This was no doubt to counter the local nature of the false teaching. The concept fits the theme of Christ as Creator and sustainer of all things in 1:15-20. If Christ rules all creatures, then all should heed the message of their Sovereign. And if "all things" are reconciled through Christ, then he must be proclaimed everywhere for that program to be realized.

and of which I, Paul, have become a servant.

"I, Paul" indicates that Timothy's name in 1:1 is not to be understood in the sense of authorship. Paul, in calling himself a servant, put himself on the same footing as Epaphras (1:7) and Tychicus (4:7).

V. PAUL'S MINISTRY TO THE CHURCHES AND
TO THE COLOSSIANS (1:24–2:5)

A. PAUL'S LABORS IN GOD'S POWER (1:24-29)

[24]Now I rejoice in what was suffered for you, and I fill up in my flesh what is still lacking in regard to Christ's afflictions, for the sake of his body, which is the church. [25]I have become its servant by the commission God gave me to present to you the word of God in its fullness — [26]the mystery that has been kept hidden for ages and generations, but is now disclosed to the saints. [27]To them God has chosen to make known among the Gentiles the glorious riches of this mystery, which is Christ in you, the hope of glory. [28]We proclaim him, admonishing and teaching everyone with all wisdom, so that we may present everyone perfect in Christ. [29]To this end I labor, struggling with all his energy, which so powerfully works in me.

Paul called himself a servant in verse 23, and he enlarges on that in the following verses. He stresses God as the source of his message and as the one who commissioned him. In describing his work he employs a number of terms that doubtless characterized the heresy, but he relates the terms to Christ. His ultimate purpose was to keep his readers from being deceived and led away from Christ (2:4,8).

1:24 Now I rejoice in what was suffered for you, and I fill up in my flesh what is still lacking in regard to Christ's afflictions, for the sake of his body, which is the church.
This verse has been one of the most puzzling in Colossians because it speaks of filling what was lacking of Christ's afflictions. Bypassing that for the moment, Paul paralleled his fleshly suffering with Christ's (v. 22). Jesus died for the Colossians, and Paul suffered for them. This lent urgency to his ministry and to his appeal that they not be drawn away from Christ. For Paul the discomfort of suffering was transcended by the joy of

bringing men reconciliation with God. From the first Paul knew he would suffer (Acts 9:16), and it was a continual feature of his ministry (cf. 1 Cor 4:9-13; 2 Cor 11:23-33; Gal 6:17).

Paul suffered for the Colossians (and for the Laodiceans, 2:1f). We are not told how this was done. Was it some special suffering just related to them? More probably he meant that all his suffering for the church was for them as well as for anyone else. Could suffering include inner agony experienced because of the threat to the church? Verses 26-29 may indicate it was related to preaching to the Gentiles.

As indicated above, the interpretive puzzle here centers in the statements "fill up" (ἀνταναπληρῶ, antanaplērō) and "lacking" (ὑστέρημα, hysterēma) in regard to Christ's afflictions. O'Brien gives an admirable summary and critique of the various interpretations:[3]

1) Paul filled a lack in the vicarious sufferings of Christ. But this would deny the all-sufficiency of Christ's sacrifice, which the New Testament strongly affirms.

2) Paul suffered "for the sake of Christ." This was true but it leaves "fill up" and "lacking" unexplained.

3) The same objection applies to the view that Paul's sufferings resembled those of Christ.

4) Paul suffered Christ's afflictions because he was in a mystical fellowship with Christ, and this would in some way benefit the church. Besides the problem of establishing a "mystical fellowship" from Paul's writings, this position also fails to adequately explain "fill up" and "lacking." Yet without going to mystical extremes, there could be a sense in which Christian suffering would "complete" the suffering of Christ.

5) Paul was employing apocalyptic language. Verse 26, and 2:2,3 employ language that has an apocalyptic sound. Building on Daniel 12:1, Jewish literature pictured the end time as being accompanied or preceded by suffering and catastrophe, which would afflict even the faithful. Those assuming that Christianity was influenced by this perspective pull into its orbit such texts

---

[3]O'Brien, *Colossians*, pp. 77-80.

about suffering as Acts 14:22 (which uses the Greek term translated "affliction" here), Mark 13:19-24 (and parallels), 1 Thessalonians 3:3,7, and Romans 8:17f, 38f. It is also held that God would limit these end time afflictions (the amount of suffering was predetermined), which would be related to the "filling up" of the present text. Thus Paul would be helping complete the Messianic woes to precede the end.

Paul has no doubt employed language familiar in apocalyptic writing. Exegesis of the passages cited, however, could challenge the use to which this position puts them. Were these passages truly apocalyptic? And what were the Christian views of the end time? In one sense it had already come (1:13f; 3:3) though there was still the Second Coming (3:4). O'Brien objects, too, to the concept of a predetermined amount of suffering.

Beyond these theories, we believe Paul was primarily concerned that the Colossians be encouraged and understand Christ, God's mystery (2:2). To accomplish this he had suffered. He may be saying that the task of proclaiming the gospel would frequently (perhaps not inevitably) involve affliction. No matter. The greater work was being done (cf. Rom 8:18). The task, thus the affliction, would go on to the end. Without preaching, the death of Christ would not have been known to unsaved humanity. Perhaps in spreading the message Christ's afflictions would be filled in that their meaning would be made known. As the preachers were afflicted, so would Christ be (Acts 9:4). It has been suggested that the particular affliction to which Paul referred here was reaction by Jews to his preaching to Gentiles, and verses 26-29 would support this. This statement of dedication, resultant from God's commission (v. 25) gave a personal dimension (in addition to the doctrinal) to Paul's case against the false teaching at Colosse.

1:25 I have become its servant by the commission God gave me to present to you the word of God in its fullness —

The word translated "commission" (οἰκονομία, *oikonomia*), often used in tandem with "mystery," was probably Paul's call by God to preach, especially to the Gentiles. The commission gave him insight into the mystery, and involved him as a "servant." Presenting the Word of God in "fullness" roughly parallels the language of Romans 15:19 (in both cases Paul uses the verb "fill up" [πληρόω, *pleroō*]) and seems to imply the complete message that was preached to the entire world, particularly to Gentiles. The fullness of preaching led to the fullness of life in Christ (cf. 1:9; 2:10).

1:26 the mystery that has been kept hidden for ages and generations, but is now disclosed to the saints.

The word of God was the "mystery" (μυστήριον, *mystērion*). If the mystery (acceptance of Gentiles) had not been preached, then the word of God would not have been proclaimed in fullness (v. 25). "Mystery" is used by Paul three times as often as in all the rest of the New Testament. It was a term, known in the Semitic world, which indicated something hidden and unknown. God would make it known in his time. So Paul asserts God had done just that, and the reality hidden so long was the acceptance of Gentiles into his community in equal standing with Jews. Not only was the mystery revealed, it was to be among the nations (v. 27) since it affected them directly. But it was grasped by the saints, the believers, since they had responded to its offer of deliverance from the "dominion of darkness" (1:13). Other references to the mystery are found in Romans 16:25; Ephesians 1:9; 3:3,4,9; 6:19; and Colossians 2:2; 4:3. Use of the term here may have been to give it its Christian meaning, contrary to any meaning the heresy may have accorded to it.

1:27 To them God has chosen to make known among the Gentiles the glorious riches of this mystery,

The veil is lifted, and the identity of the mystery appears — gloriously (cf. 2:2f; Eph 1:7,18; 3:8,16)! God's choice had led to Paul's commission (v. 24). The Old Testament does indicate that God's plan was ultimately for all men (Gen 12:3; Isa 49:6), but the manner and time of it were not in the way it was anticipated by the Jews. Thus we witness the early struggles in the church regarding Gentiles becoming Jews before they could become Christians (Acts 15; Galatians).

which is Christ in you, the hope of glory.

"Christ in you" could refer to the fact Christ was preached to Gentiles, or, less likely in this context, to the indwelling Christ in the life of each Christian. If parallel to "among the Gentiles" it would mean "among" you. On hope cf. 1:5,22. Paul refers to the "glory" in 3:4. It will come when Christ appears, and we see the magnificent culmination of the believer's pilgrimage.

1:28 We proclaim him, admonishing and teaching everyone with all wisdom, so that we may present everyone perfect in Christ.

This further description of the Christian ministry seems expressed in particular opposition to the false teaching. "Wisdom" (σοφία, *sophia*) and "perfect" (τέλειος, *teleios*) may both be terms which the heretics connected with their philosophy. Paul connects them with Christ. If the false teachers promulgated a view for the "spiritually elite," Paul's threefold use of the expression "all men" (in the Greek; NIV "everyone") combatted that by indicating the universality of Christ's offer of salvation.

Paul's proclamation includes admonition (lit. "setting in order") and teaching. The same two terms occur in 3:16. Wisdom here is practical, referring to the manner of preaching. Cf. another practical application in 4:5. Paul's wisdom in preaching can be verified from 1 Corinthians 9:23ff, and from his delicate treatment of the matter of Onesimus in Philemon. His goal was to present everyone perfect in Christ, similar to the statement of verse 22. Here the Second Coming seems to be the occasion meant.

1:29 To this end I labor,

In verse 28 the first person plural was used as Paul included his associates, but here he speaks of his personal activity. As he

suffered for the Colossians (v. 24), now he labors. In the next
verse he relates his efforts specifically to the Colossians.
Though Paul was a prisoner this did not diminish the fire within him to do God's work. Later he asked the Colossians to pray
for an opportunity for him to preach (4:2-4).

**struggling with all his energy, which so powerfully works in
me.**
Two strong impressions arise from this verse. The first is
Paul's intensity, reflected in the words "labor" (κοπιάω, *kopiaō*)
and "struggling" (from ἀγωνίζομαι, *agōnizomai*). The first indicates severe labor (cf. 1 Cor 4:12; 15:10; Phil 2:16). The latter
is an intensive form of the Greek term from which our "agony"
comes. But beyond this depiction of extreme effort is grace.
God's power was at work within Paul. Twice in the Greek he
used the term ἐνεργεία (*energeia*) from which "energy" is
derived, and once he used δύναμις (*dynamis*, root of dynamic,
dynamite, etc.). On this power see 1:11; 2:12 and cf. Ephesians
1:19; 3:7,16,20; and 6:10. Divine empowering made possible
Paul's great devotion to his mission. Work and grace go hand
in hand.

COLOSSIANS 2

B. WARNING AGAINST BEING DECEIVED (2:1-5)

¹I want you to know how much I am struggling for you and for those at Laodicea, and for all who have not met me personally. ²My purpose is that they may be encouraged in heart and united in love, so that they may have the full riches of complete understanding, in order that they may know the mystery of God, namely, Christ, ³in whom are hidden all the treasures of wisdom and knowledge. ⁴I tell you this so that no one may deceive you by fine-sounding arguments. ⁵For though I am absent from you in body, I am present with you in spirit and delight to see how orderly you are and how firm your faith in Christ is.

2:1 I want you to know how much I am struggling for you and for those at Laodicea, and for all who have not met me personally.

Though he had not seen the Colossians or the Laodiceans, Paul did not wish this to be a disadvantage. So he describes his struggles for them. He uses the noun form ("how great a *struggle* I have") of the verb *agōnizomai* found in the previous verse. The struggle was no doubt the preaching of Christ, here especially as teaching, admonition (1:28), and encouragement toward fuller understanding (2:2). The battle against the threatened inroads of heresy could be part of the specific struggle here.

The reference to Laodicea may indicate that the heresy threatened them as well (cf. 4:13,16). "All who have not met me personally" might refer to others in the Lycus Valley (Hierapolis, 4:13?). If it is understood generally as "any one, anywhere" it would weaken the personal appeal of these words.

2:2 My purpose is that they may be encouraged in heart and united in love,

Paul continues to apply themes to his readers in specific ways which he has previously noted in a general way. "United in love" is a call to the virtue which binds "all together" (3:14) and which was inspired by God's love for them (3:12). Thus we see the contrast of the unitive love in Christ with the divisive effects of the false teaching. Another interpretation of "united" sees the word as referring to instructions. Then the reference would be to Paul's teaching method.

so that they may have the full riches of complete understanding,

"Understanding" (σύνεσις, *synesis*) echoes the prayer of 1:9. This fullness (here πληροφορία, *plērophoria*, "full assurance") had been addressed in 1:15-20, and awaits further amplification in 2:9-15. When this had been grasped, the emptiness of the heresy would be evident. This understanding would be personal, through being in relationship with Christ. Paul was certainly going beyond mere cognition here.

in order that they may know the mystery of God, namely, Christ,

The last of the verse is confusing in the original Greek. It is, literally, "the mystery of God, Christ." The NIV seems to catch the viewpoint most widely held and most closely conformed to the context. On "mystery" see the notes on 1:26.

2:3 in whom are hidden all the treasures of wisdom and knowledge.

Christ is a treasury whence understanding derives its riches. "Hidden" (ἀπόκρυφοι, *apokryphoi*) could not mean inaccessible, for then the text would be senseless, and would contradict 1:26. Rather, it refers to the place the treasures were stored. Others may claim to find the treasure elsewhere, but "all" indicates the futility of their quest. Any other so-called treasure was incomparable to Christ.

It has been observed that Paul uses typical Jewish terminology in this verse, as some feel was the case in 1:15-18. Thus it is suggested he may be confuting the Jewish element of the heresy (cf. vv. 16f) by using its own language.

2:4 I tell you this so that no one may deceive you

Paul comes at last to a direct warning. His foundation has been so well laid no reader would want to be beguiled. The strength of the appeal here can be appreciated by reviewing all that the letter has said previously about Christ. And the verses to come will make it stronger yet.

by fine-sounding arguments.

"Fine-sounding" (πιθανολογία, *pithanologia*) was a term used in philosophic discussions for arguments that lacked certainty. Weed suggests a meaning like the modern "fast talk."[1] It had to do with persuasive speech, directed the wrong way. But it did sound good, which made it dangerous.

2:5 For though I am absent from you in body, I am present with you in spirit

Paul, away, knew danger lurked. Though he complimented them with the words "orderly" and "firm," it was never too early to warn about an impending problem. Indeed it would seem that the problem was in some way present but that the church had not yet been affected negatively. Their stability gave Paul good ground on which to rest his exhortations. Their case demonstrates that there is no better defense against heresy than a proper understanding of Christ, both in thought and action.

---

[1]Michael Weed, *The Letters of Paul to the Ephesians, Colossians, and Philemon* (Austin: Sweet, 1971), p. 65.

and delight to see how orderly you are and how firm your faith in Christ is.

"How orderly you are" is rendered "your morale" in the NRSV. In some usages "order" (τάξις, *taxis*) and "firmness" (στερέωμα, *stereōma*) referred to military ranks lined up solidly before the enemy. It is debated whether Paul had this image in mind here. It does not affect the basic meaning of the passage, however.

VI. RECEIVING CHRIST AS LORD (2:6-15)

A. CONTINUE IN CHRIST: DON'T BE DECEIVED! (2:6-8)

⁶So then, just as you received Christ Jesus as Lord, continue to live in him, ⁷rooted and built up in him, strengthened in the faith as you were taught, and overflowing with thankfulness.

⁸See to it that no one takes you captive through hollow and deceptive philosophy, which depends on human tradition and the basic principles of this world rather than on Christ.

2:6 So then, just as you received Christ Jesus as Lord, continue to live in him,

Verses 6 and 7 are transitional, catching up ideas Paul has set forth previously, preparatory to his climactic depiction of the blessedness of life in Christ and his assault on the heresy. On Christ and his relationship to men see 1:10,15-20,23 and 27. The reception of Christ may refer to Epaphras' original evangelistic work. The reference to the Lordship of Christ derives its impact from 1:15-20. "Continue to live," in imperative form (περιπατεῖτε, *peripateite*, lit. "walk"), reaffirms "orderly" and "firm" of verse 5. How could the Colossians contemplate not living "in him," given all Paul had said?

2:7 rooted and built up in him, strengthened in the faith as you were taught, and overflowing with thankfulness.

Four participles are used by Paul to support "continue to

live." O'Brien points out that the first three are all passive, indicating what had been done for the Colossians and what they were to retain.[2] The fourth (περισσεύοντες, *perisseuontes*, "overflowing") describes what they should continue to do. "Rooted" (ἐρριζωμένοι, *errizōmenoi*) is perfect tense — a settled condition — while the next three are present — "now and continuing." "Rooted" is agricultural (cf. Eph 3:17). "Built up" (ἐποικοδομούμενοι, *epoikodomoumenoi*) is architectural (cf. 2 Cor 10:8; 1 Thess 5:11). "Strengthened" (βεβαιούμενοι, *bebaioumenoi*) may be a legal term, indicating the guarantee of a contract (cf. 1 Cor 1:8). "The faith" is probably the Christian teaching which they had received, though some hold it to be one's personal faith. "Thankfulness" is the great motivator to Christian behavior, and is a theme often noted in Colossians (1:3,12; 3:15,16,17; and 4:2).

2:8 See to it that no one takes you captive through hollow and deceptive philosophy, which depends on human tradition

From 2:8 to 3:4 Paul addresses the heresy directly, presenting it in strong contrast to what Christ has done for men. There is no indication the false teachers wished to abandon Christ. For them it was "Christ and . . . ." So Paul demonstrates there could be no "Christ and . . . ," but just "Christ only!"

In this section there are 15 words found only here in the New Testament (of 34 such words in Colossians). There are 21 words in this section that are used less than 5 times in the New Testament (of 64 such words in Colossians). Thus the vocabulary of these verses is not typical of Paul's writings. This may be because he was employing the language of the false teachers to turn it against them in refutation.

Συλαγωγέω (*sylagōgeō*, "carry off"; NIV "take captive"), one of these unique words, warns them not to be led off as a looter might carry off booty. The "deceivers" of verse 4 are the "looters" here. "Philosophy," though only in this form in the New Testament, was a term widely used in the ancient world,

---

[2]O'Brien, *Colossians*, p. 106.

by both Greeks and Jews. It had no inherently bad connota-tion, and may have been a word used to describe the heresy. Paul modified it by "hollow" and "deceptive," words carrying a powerful condemnation, especially in combination with the other language of this verse. "Tradition" (παράδοσις, *paradosis*, "giving over") implied something handed down from the past, and often gave an air of respect and authority to its contents. So it was "tradition" (heretical) versus "tradition" (Christian). Paul dubbed the one "human" to carry his point. It was really man's word against God's gospel.

and the basic principles of this world rather than on Christ.

The most troublesome interpretative problem here is deter-mining the meaning of "basic principles" (στοιχεῖα, *stoicheia*). The root meaning of the word was "that which is found in a series."[3] In some usages it referred to "earth, wind, fire and water." It also described the letters of the alphabet, in order; or the principles on which all else was built; or the basic ele-ments of which the world was made. Thus as a reference to basic elements the term could have one of a variety of mean-ings. The word is also found in Colossians 2:20, and elsewhere in the New Testament in Galatians 4:3, 9; Hebrews 5:12; 2 Peter 3:10,12, but none of the New Testament usages gives a completely clear meaning applicable to this text.

What does *stoicheia* mean here? O'Brien lists three major lines of interpretation.[4] A first sees *stoicheia* as principles of religious instruction in the world prior to Christ, as if the heretics were returning to an immature stage of religion. A second considers the meaning to be the elements of the visible material world, and would argue the heresy tried to bind adherents to things of this world. The third, and most widely accepted view today, sees *stoicheia* as personal spiritual beings who would control access to God (in the heresy). They would

---

[3]Petr Pokorný, *Colossians, A Commentary* (Peabody, MA: Hendrickson, 1991), p. 113.

[4]O'Brien, *Colossians*, pp. 130-132.

be the same as the "powers and authorities" of 2:10,15. In some way, then, the attempt was made to relate to these powers. It is objected that this view does not parallel "human tradition." One study (Wink) has argued that no case of this meaning for the term can be clearly documented before the third century A.D.[5] However this does not prove the term could not have been used that way earlier.

The problem is a puzzling one. Paul was probably quoting the false teachers here. Whatever they meant, Paul's "of this world" with the earlier "human" makes their case a pitiful rival to Christ, as the following verses will powerfully demonstrate.

B. "IN CHRIST" (2:9-12)

[9]For in Christ all the fullness of the Deity lives in bodily form, [10]and you have been given fullness in Christ, who is the head over every power and authority. [11]In him you were also circumcised, in the putting off of the sinful nature,[a] not with a circumcision done by the hands of men but with the circumcision done by Christ, [12]having been buried with him in baptism and raised with him through your faith in the power of God, who raised him from the dead.

[a]*11 Or the flesh*

2:9 For in Christ all the fullness of the Deity lives in bodily form,

The heretics did not attack faith in Christ, but failed to recognize the real meaning and implications of that faith. This Paul now sets forth. This verse repeats the Christ hymn (1:19) with the addition of "bodily." "In Christ" is literally "in him." "Fullness" (πλήρωμα, *plērōma*) can mean that Christ was God in every sense save for the necessary bounds of human limitation.

---

[5]Cited in Arthur Patzia, *Ephesians, Colossians, Philemon* (Peabody, MA: Hendrickson, 1984), pp. 53f.

Melick says "Jesus is every bit God."[6] Or, in this context it may primarily indicate the complete working of God to bring salvation. "Deity" is from a Greek term (θεότης, *theotēs*) only here in the New Testament, and indicates the very nature of God.

The problematic part of this verse concerns the meaning of "dwells bodily." Many conjectures have been offered. We believe it refers to the incarnation. Since "dwells" is in the present tense it indicates the risen Christ is still the fullness of deity as savior, as he was upon earth. The significance of the incarnation continues.

Since Christ is the fullness, then the benefits of God's saving grace are to be found nowhere else. The next verse moves on to this point.

2:10 and you have been given fullness in Christ,

In a remarkable parallel the fullness motif continues. Christians have fullness in Christ. The meaning would need to be understood in a way appropriate to the situation and need, since it obviously could not be fullness in exactly the same sense as with Christ. "Fullness" here would certainly mean forgiveness, life, and victory over any hostile powers, as verses 13-15 indicate. It no doubt means even more than that, quite beyond human comprehension (cf. John 1:16). Fullness once again underlines the all-sufficiency of Christ.

who is the head over every power and authority.

On power and authority see 1:16f and 2:15. As Christ was head of the church (1:18), he is head of all entities. He will determine their destiny, and ultimately they cannot resist his headship.

2:11 In him you were also circumcised,

Fullness is described by a number of terms in verses 11-13. In traveling from fullness to baptism Paul passed through circumci-

---

[6]Richard Melick, *Philippians, Colossians, Philemon* (Nashville: Broadman, 1991), p. 255.

sion. Why this image? Some suggest the heretics had a circumcision requirement (cf. other aspects of Judaism in v. 16). This was
unlikely since Paul said nothing about it, compared to letters like
Galatians where his concern was raised so high.

in the putting off of the sinful nature,

As the NIV understands the passage the removal of sin by
Christ is compared to the removal of the male foreskin in circumcision. Perhaps an intermediate parallel would be the
removal of the garments at baptism. Then in the baptismal
burial there would be the death to sin, followed by the resurrection to new life. Baptism was the instrument of sin's
removal, though certainly the immersion in water, *per se*, did
not save. Paul gave a spiritual sense to circumcision also in
Romans 2:28 and Philippians 3:3. This usage has Old Testament antecedents (Deuteronomy 10:16; 30:6; Jeremiah 4:4).
Circumcision implies a divine ordinance (Gen 17:9-14) and the
"new" circumcision indicates a new stage in God's dealing with
men. The covenant sign for Israel, newly interpreted, has now
become appropriate as a covenant sign for all men. Yet we
should not push Paul's words beyond his intent. The fact that
circumcision was administered to infants cannot be taken to
argue for infant baptism. That would introduce a conclusion
beyond the intent of the Apostle's argument. Not only does
the verse describe the removal of sin, it is an indirect exhortation to live a life free of sin. Further, the circumcision image
may say that this was the way the body of flesh was put off,
rather than by asceticism.

not with a circumcision done by the hands of men but with the circumcision done by Christ,

An alternative, and we believe less likely, interpretation has
been offered. Christ is the subject and the circumcision was his
circumcision. This view relies partly on a parallel with 1:22,
and indicates Christ's death as well. "Putting off the sinful
nature" which in the NIV is an interpretive translation, is given
the literal meaning of putting off "the flesh." This is taken to

refer to the death of Christ. On this view, then, verse 12 completes the progression through burial and resurrection. Objectors point out that this is a bizarre way of referring to Christ's death, contrasted to the clarity of 1:22, and that there is no specific reference to Christ's death as in 1:22 ("Christ's" in the NIV is "his" in Greek). Also the language would seem to diminish the importance of the resurrection, since Christ was still in his body then. Further, the thrust of these verses was blessings to Christians.

We can sum the context as follows. In Christ is God's fullness bodily. In the church, Christ's body, Christians find fullness. This fullness involves putting off the body of flesh (sin).

2:12 having been buried with him in baptism and raised with him through your faith

In Romans 6:1-4 (the only other passage using language similar to this) baptism is specifically connected with death. Here death is not mentioned, but is clearly implied by "buried," since only corpses are buried. But the greater stress in this verse is on resurrection. Though the final resurrection of the body was to come (3:4), there is no contradiction here to that. The two fit smoothly into the one system, if the nature of each is known. Between the two stands the call to faithful service which fills the New Testament, and the danger of apostasy (cf. 1 Cor 10:1-13).

in the power of God, who raised him from the dead.

Normally the power of God refers to that which is given by God to the Christian. Here it is what the Christian believes, but probably also implies the further power of God that characterized Christian experience. It would be a risk to volunteer to die unless there were hope of resurrection. Note the paradox here with verse 10 — "fullness." In Christ is fullness in death.

This text is pivotal in the book. Throughout readers are called to a deeper understanding and practice of the commitment they have made to Christ. It is clear that they all had been baptized, and that it was at that point the transition from death to life was made. This is not to imply water or works salvation, nor to discount faith, but to say that this act, symbolic of what happened to Christ, was a "rite of passage" from the old life to the new. As one author has noted, in baptism God chose to make something happen. Otherwise Paul's words make no sense. Baptism is like the neck of the hourglass, through which the sand must pass to go from one end to the other.

C. DEATH TO LIFE (2:13-15)

[13]**When you were dead in your sins and in the uncircumcision of your sinful nature,[a] God made you alive with Christ. He forgave us all our sins, [14]having canceled the written code, with its regulations, that was against us and that stood opposed to us; he took it away, nailing it to the cross. [15]And having disarmed the powers and authorities, he made a public spectacle of them, triumphing over them by the cross.[b]**

[a]*13 Or your flesh*   [b]*15 Or them in him*

2:13 When you were dead in your sins and in the uncircumcision of your sinful nature,

Paul describes their pre-baptism life, and repeats the images of the two previous verses. Death (by implication) with Christ (from v. 12) delivers from death in sin. In other words, death is inevitable, but one could choose one's death (in sin or to sin). "Uncircumcised" picks up verse 11. Here it seems to have two senses; as Gentiles, and as unredeemed persons, with the latter the more significant. The Greek term rendered "sins" (παραπτώματα, *paraptōmata*) is not the usual word (it literally means "false step") but there seems no difference in significance.

God made you alive with Christ.

Dead men cannot bring themselves to life, nor could those dead in sin achieve their own forgiveness. The "sheer grace" of

God pictured here is an effective counter to any requirements the false teachers suggested were necessary for salvation. Forgiveness is finally specified in the last part of the verse, though implied throughout the paragraph.

He forgave us all our sins,

Because of the style of verses 13c-15, with the large number of uncharacteristically Pauline words, some think they may be a confession of faith from the life of the church which Paul has employed here to suit his purposes.

2:14 having canceled the written code, with its regulations, that was against us and that stood opposed to us; he took it away, nailing it to the cross.

God has taken away sin by Jesus' death on the cross. Both the debt and the document recording it were destroyed. Note how Paul emphasizes this with "canceled," "take it away," and "nailed." Thus we have obliteration, deportation and nailing, which may bear some relation to the charges against Christ, or to Jesus' body itself as it was nailed to the cross. But what is the meaning of "written code" and "regulations" which Paul (perhaps from a church confession) used here? And why did Paul choose this way of making his point? It may have been a specific refutation dealing with the Jewish regulations of verse 16, as well as with the "regulations" of verse 20.

"Written code" comes from a word (χειρόγραφον, *cheirographon*) meaning, literally, "handwriting." It meant a document designating an obligation. The idea of a divine accounting of man's debts was familiar to the Judaism of the day. To what did it refer? We consider the most likely view to be any code of conduct under which a man stood, but which he could not keep. For the Jew this would be the Law of Moses (Gal 3:10,12). For Gentiles it would be the moral law, however understood (cf. Rom 2:12-15). The code of conduct, not perfectly obeyed, would have penalties. Ultimately the failure would be failure to obey God. Thus one was locked into condemnation, save for grace (v. 13, and cf. Gal 3:24f; Rom

3:21ff). Now Christians were free from the condemnation of the document, though not free from responsibility (cf. 3:1-4).

2:15 And having disarmed the powers and authorities, he made a public spectacle of them,

Another consequence or blessing of Christ's death and resurrection was making the "powers and authorities" into a "spectacle." Paul had already asserted that they owed their origin to Christ (1:16) and that he was their head (2:10).

Two interpretive problems occur here, concerning first, the subject of the verse, and second, the meaning of the word translated "disarmed" (from ἀπεκδύω, *apekduō*). Is God or Christ the subject here? The natural sense seems to be God, going back to verse 13, "God made you alive." God, then, disarmed and humiliated the powers and authorities, but did it through Christ.

triumphing over them by the cross.

The view that Christ was the subject is interwoven with the meaning of "disarmed." Those arguing this position say the subject changed to Christ in verse 14. The verb "disarmed" is in the middle voice, picturing the subject acting on or for himself. Thus it is held that Christ divested himself of the "powers" by his death, and the last part of the verse is translated "in him" to support this. "By the cross" of the NIV is an interpretive translation of the Greek, which can be rendered "in it," and legitimately refer to the cross.

The view that Christ is the subject goes against the natural sense of the passage. The middle voice can also be translated as active. Further there is no indication that Christ had to divest himself of the powers and authorities, though one might see them as having the power to cause his death.

However understood, the powers that led Jesus to death were vanquished by their very deed and the subsequent resurrection. Now, humiliated and powerless, they were publicly displayed as victims. The image is of the captives in a triumphal return procession of soldiers.

VII. WARNINGS AGAINST THE HERESY (2:16-23)

A. DON'T LOSE THE PRIZE! (2:16-19)

¹⁶Therefore do not let anyone judge you by what you eat or drink, or with regard to a religious festival, a New Moon celebration or a Sabbath day. ¹⁷These are a shadow of the things that were to come; the reality, however, is found in Christ. ¹⁸Do not let anyone who delights in false humility and the worship of angels disqualify you for the prize. Such a person goes into great detail about what he has seen, and his unspiritual mind puffs him up with idle notions. ¹⁹He has lost connection with the Head, from whom the whole body, supported and held together by its ligaments and sinews, grows as God causes it to grow.

2:16 Therefore do not let anyone judge you by what you eat or drink,

The "philosophy" of 2:8 is now described, though to the modern reader much still remains unclear. The Colossians could no doubt "fill in the gaps" by their understanding of their local situation. It is difficult to meld the elements described in verses 16-23 into a coherent whole. It would seem there was no intent to deny Christ, but rather to "add" to faith in him. The best antidote to this, as Paul has so powerfully demonstrated to this point, was to truly understand Christ and his work. We cannot fully know just what specific perception the false teachers had of Christ.

Paul tells the Colossians not to worry about judgment or disqualification (v. 18) from the heretics, who would judge by the "basic principles" of verse 20 (see discussion on 2:8). To submit to the regulations would be to submit to the wrong powers.

It is assumed that the heretics forbade food and drink, and required the observance of holy days. These items appear at first to be aspects of Judaism, and one might suspect the same problem that plagued the Galatian churches — the attempt to bind the Law of Moses on Gentiles. "Drink," however, creates a problem, since there were no Jewish prohibitions at this point (Lev 10:9; 11:34,36 and Num 6:3 were special cases). Thus some have suggested these were non-Jewish ascetic regulations (cf. vv. 21,23), perhaps practiced to prepare for divine revelation (worship of angels — v. 18?) or for some other reason. Lohse notes, for example, that ancients could abstain from meat to achieve purity.[7] Cf. also 1 Timothy 4:3.

or with regard to a religious festival, a New Moon celebration or a Sabbath day.

The festivals, celebrations and sabbaths (v. 17) seem to refer to annual, monthly and weekly Jewish observances. Paul does not condemn their observance *per se*, but does argue against them as prompted by the στοιχεῖα (*stoicheia*, v. 20) and as items necessary for salvation. He makes this clear in verse 17. It appears from the present verse that a strange mixture of Jewish and pagan elements characterized the "philosophy" Paul was combatting. One provocative view suggests that the heretics held that supernatural powers stood behind the seasonal changes which the festivals, etc., celebrated. However, it is hard to think Paul would be silent about it if that were the case.

2:17 These are a shadow of the things that were to come; the reality, however, is found in Christ.

"Shadow" depicts a transitory thing, but it did relate to what would come. Thus it would seem that the holy days, at least, were Jewish (cf. Heb 8:5, 10:1). But the old foretold the new. "Reality" translates σῶμα (*sōma*), the usual word for body. But the *sōma* was Christ himself. It is possible both Paul and the heretics agreed the items of verse 16 were shadows. They would differ, presumably, regarding the identity of the "reality."

---

[7]Eduard Lohse, *Colossians and Philippians* (Philadelphia: Fortress, 1971), p. 115.

2:18 Do not let anyone who delights in false humility and the worship of angels disqualify you for the prize.

In a difficult section of the book this verse is the most difficult. A comparison of English translations indicates something of the problems. And even when the Greek has been translated the question of its meaning remains. In our discussion we rely heavily on O'Brien, who in turn discusses the view of Francis in detail (F.O. Francis, "Humility and Angelic Worship in 2:18," in *Conflict at Colossae*).[8]

The verse opens in Greek with Paul's warning about disqualification. It would appear the heretics maintained an air of superiority toward others (humility notwithstanding). But to follow their practices would keep one from the prize, as the NIV renders it. However, "for the prize" is not in the Greek, so the NIV again translates interpretively. In following Christ there could be no disqualification, since he embodied total reality. Another way of seeing this verse would be to translate "condemn" or "judge" (as in v. 16) instead of "disqualify," with the sense that the heretics condemned those who did not share in their practices.

The expression "false humility" is actually only the word for "humility" (ταπεινοφροσύνη, *tapeinophrosynē*), and is the same term that describes a virtue in 3:12. Given the context, and "puffs up" later in the verse, "false" may be an appropriate addition, and the idea is found in other translations than the NIV. It could describe the zeal and submissiveness with which the adherents practiced the heretical activities. Another possibility is suggested by Francis, who cites parallels to instances where the term indicated fasts and other sorts of self-denial (as in v. 21) which were believed to enhance visions of "heavenly mysteries." This view does make a logical connection with verses 20-23.

"Worship of angels" is generally understood as the praise directed to beings less than God. But Francis suggests the Greek is to be understood as the worship which angels them-

---

[8]O'Brien, *Colossians*, pp. 141-146.

selves performed (subjective genitive) and he supports this from Jewish (nonbiblical) literature. The meaning, then, would be an exalted experience in which the practitioners would either observe or participate in the angelic worship of God. This would be some type of visionary experience.

Such a person goes into great detail about what he has seen, and his unspiritual mind puffs him up with idle notions.
The next expression in Greek is the most difficult in the verse. The NIV has "goes into great detail about what he has seen," and the NRSV has "dwelling on visions." The literal translation is "which he has seen upon entering," and the problematic word is that translated "entering." The word ἐμβατεύω (*embateuō*) can be rendered "to set foot upon," "enter," "come into possession of," or "enter into a subject" (with the idea of investigation). Numerous interpretations of the meaning have been offered. Dibelius understood it as paralleling the rites of the mystery religions, but this view lacks corroborative evidence from elsewhere in Colossians. Others think it refers to investigating what was seen in a vision. Francis thinks the "seen" was the mental vision of the angels worshiping God, and that the "entering" was the worshipers coming into the heavenly realm and the worship taking place there through that vision. Despite the difficulties the verse refers to a mystical, esoteric spiritual experience, probably available only to a few, which doubtless made those who experienced it convinced they were of a higher level of relationship to God. To them salvation through Christ was not enough. They had to be saved by this mysterious "more."

Whatever their estimates of themselves and their experiences, Paul delivered a telling blow when he told them they were puffed up with idle notions, and that their mental state, rather than being deeply in tune with things divine, was really "unspiritual." The Greek τοῦ νοὸς τῆς σαρκός (*tou noös tēs sarkos*) is literally "mind of the flesh," and a fleshly mind often refers to that which is opposed to God (cf. Rom 8:5f). They may have felt themselves exalted and "super-spiritual." In reality they were most conceited and unspiritual. What a devastating judgment, the more so when considered over against their self-estimate!

2:19 He has lost connection with the Head, from whom the whole body, supported and held together by its ligaments and sinews, grows as God causes it to grow.

Perhaps one could argue that the additional activities described in verses 16-18 did not destroy discipleship to Christ. Paul dispelled that notion. It was an "either/or," not a "both/and." In describing Christ as Head, source of unity and nourishment and avenue of divinely produced growth, Paul painted, by contrast, a miserable picture of the heretics. They had no relation to Christ, despite any claims they may have made. They had no divine source of nourishment ("supported"; from ἐπιχορηγέω, *epichorēgeō*, "supply/furnish") or unity ("held together"; from συμβιβάζω, *symbibazō*, the same verb as "united" in 2:2). They were spiritually starved, despite their claims, and divisive. Since they were cut off from nourishment, they did not have the possibility of growth. They were stunted, and whatever they might have considered growth was not growth at all. These "puffed up" people were pathetic creatures indeed, claiming burgeoning health when actually suffering starvation.

B. SHUN WORLDLY RULES! (2:20-23)

[20]**Since you died with Christ to the basic principles of this world, why, as though you still belonged to it, do you submit to its rules:** [21]**"Do not handle! Do not taste! Do not touch!"?** [22]**These are all destined to perish with use, because they are based on human commands and teachings.** [23]**Such regulations indeed have an appearance of wisdom, with their self-imposed worship, their false humility and their harsh treatment of the body, but they lack any value in restraining sensual indulgence.**

2:20 Since you died with Christ to the basic principles of this world,

Not only had the heretics lost connection with the head, those truly in Christ had died to such "basic principles." Death with Christ was accomplished in baptism (v. 12, and cf. Rom 6:1-4). The heretics were not living out the consequences of their baptism. On "basic principles" cf. the discussion at 2:8. The understanding of this text depends on how the term is interpreted; whether it means spiritual powers or the elements of worldly life apart from Christ. If the latter, Paul may have meant that the appearance of spiritual excellence in the heresy was really a disguised form of the old life, before Christ. Perhaps this was because human will and desire were placed ahead of submission of Christ.

why, as though you still belonged to it, do you submit to its rules:

"Rules" (a form of δογματίζω, *dogmatizō*) is from the Greek root translated "regulations" in verse 14. Though not involving immoral behavior, they did involve an implicit denial that Christ's sacrifice was sufficient for salvation.

2:21 "Do not handle! Do not taste! Do not touch!"?

The NIV places these three absolute prohibitions in quotation marks, implying, correctly we think, that Paul was quoting the false teachers. These rules probably had to do with eating and drinking, as in verse 16, though it is hard to see the exact meaning of not handling or touching. Some scholars suggest a progression in the terms here, from the broadest to the narrowest meaning. ("Don't do this . . . don't even do this.") This attractive suggestion is difficult to support from the Greek, however. Some suppose there may have been subregulations under these headings. Salvation to the heretics was related to physical contact and diet. As indicated in the notes at verse 16, these prohibitions may have been intended to make possible the experience described in verse 18.

2:22 These are all destined to perish with use, because they are based on human commands and teachings.

Two criticisms are made by Paul in this verse. The first was the perishability of the material things which the heretics gave such importance, and the second was that the rules were of human origin, not divine. One's relation to God did not depend on whether one used or abstained from food and drink. Elsewhere Paul said no food was unclean in itself (Rom 14:14; 1 Cor 8:8; 10:25f; 1 Tim 4:3). The heretics rested their spiritual welfare on a material, not a spiritual, foundation. Material things were as important to them in one way as greed was to sinners in another way. In both cases the material world dictated their actions (cf. Titus 1:13-15).

2:23 Such regulations indeed

"Such regulations" is added in the NIV. This verse is very difficult in the Greek, which leads to quite opposite translations. The NIV indicates the heretical practices were valueless to restrain "sensual indulgence." Others suggest a reading which would indicate that all these things did was to gratify the flesh. In neither case is the translation smooth. Theologically both possibilities are true. External prohibitions alone did not produce godliness — it was a matter of the heart. On the other hand a religion concerned with taboos could also have the effect of indicating that all that mattered was dealing with fleshly appetites. In both cases the inner dimension of the faith would be ignored (contrast "set your hearts" in 3:1).

Another issue of interpretation is determining which language quoted the heretics and which was Paul's. Though not affecting the overall meaning of the verse, knowing this would assist in knowing when the language was straightforward, and when it had an implied criticism.

have an appearance of wisdom, with their self-imposed worship, their false humility and their harsh treatment of the body,

The "appearance of wisdom" echoes "fine sounding" of verse four. Here the translation is an interpretation of the literal "which is a word having wisdom." The NIV assumes these words were a criticism, not a quotation of the heretics. All treasures of wisdom are found in Christ (2:3). "Self-imposed worship" is translated differently in various versions. It is literally "will worship" (ἐθελοθρησκία, *ethelothrēskia*). It has been suggested this was the term used by the devotees of the heresy to indicate their free choice of the cult. Other meanings are also possible. "False" is interpolated, as in verse 18, since the Greek has only the word rendered "humility" (ταπεινοφροσύνη, *tapeinophrosynē*). "Harsh treatment" probably refers to the prohibitions of verses 16 and 21, and may indicate other ascetic practices not enumerated by Paul.

but they lack any value in restraining sensual indulgence.

The last of the verse is literally "not in a certain value toward satisfying the flesh."[9] Because it is unclear it has led some (as NIV) to indicate the regulations were ineffectual; and others argue it means that the heresy only served to gratify the flesh.

As an alternative, making the heresy pale by comparison, Paul offers 3:1-4.

---

[9]Melick, *Colossians*, p. 279.

COLOSSIANS 3

VIII. SEEK THE THINGS ABOVE (3:1-4)

¹Since, then, you have been raised with Christ, set your hearts on things above, where Christ is seated at the right hand of God. ²Set your minds on things above, not on earthly things. ³For you died, and your life is now hidden with Christ in God. ⁴When Christ, who is your[a] life, appears, then you also will appear with him in glory.

[a]4 Some manuscripts *our*

Verses 1-4 pick up many of the ideas previously set forth in Colossians, and prepare for the same ideas to be repeated later. Here was the true Christian profession, contrasted to the heresy. The false teaching is left behind, at least in terms of specific reference, and Paul moves into the ethical section of the letter. He will speak of the true heart of devotion to God, rather than the empty system he had just criticized. As these four verses center in the believer's relation to Christ, so the ethical appeals will draw their power from the relation to Christ (3:11,12,13,15,16,17,18,19,23,24).

3:1 Since, then, you have been raised with Christ, set your hearts on things above, where Christ is seated at the right hand of God.

Pokorný points out that the entire paranetic section, through 4:6, shows the importance of their baptism, since obedience was the living out of the promise and divine transformation accomplished at that time.[1] The death and resurrection motifs imply

---

[1]Pokorný, *Colossians*, p. 157.

their baptism (2:12) and are indicated as well in verses 5 and 12. It is quite likely that the convert was given ethical instruction at baptism, and this would explain the proximity of baptismal allusions and ethical exhortation.

Here Christians had been raised. Verse 4 looks forward to the ultimate resurrection. But for the present the resurrection at baptism contained moral demands. "Become what you are" was Paul's meaning. "Above" was not important spatially, but rather as the dwelling place of Christ. "Let that life be lived out in your life" (cf. 3:12-16). "Things above" were eternal, compared to things that perish (2:22). As Christ was raised and ascended, so let his risen disciples put their hearts into ascent. On "the right hand of God" see Psalm 110:1; Mark 12:36 and parallels.

3:2 Set your minds on things above, not on earthly things.

This verse seems to repeat the previous one, but there is a Greek nuance the NIV misses by using "set" in both. In verse 1 the term means to "seek" while in verse 2 a different term indicates a mind set which determines actions. The Greek here is φρονέω (*phroneō*), and the word is a favorite with Paul (cf. notes at Phil 1:7). Melick says verse 1 is moral and verse 2 is mental. Seek, and then become what you find.[2] "Earthly things" may be a parting reference to the heresy, but also anticipates 3:5-10. Christian thoughts and minds were not to be trapped by the concerns and values of the fallen order, even though Christians must live in it.

3:3 For you died,

In verses 3 and 4 the motivation for the imperatives of verses 1 and 2 are more fully unfolded. Those who were raised in their baptisms had also died. The death theme is continued with "put to death" in verse 5. As "raised" in verse 1 called for further effort, so does "died."

---

[2]Melick, *Colossians*, p. 280.

and your life is now hidden with Christ in God.

Why did Paul choose "hidden" (from κρύπτω, *kryptō*) to describe their situation with Christ? Safety and security might be implied, as well as a source of strength and well-being. Bruce says the Christian has "a doubled rampart" — with Christ in God.[3] It has also been suggested that "hidden" indicates that the source of the Christian's life is hidden from a world which does not know the Lord. Or it could be a play on some concept held by the heretics. Since the next verse speaks of appearing it may have implied that the full blessedness of the saints was not yet known.

3:4 When Christ, who is your life, appears, then you also will appear with him in glory.

As Colossians began with hope in 1:5, so the doctrinal section ends with hope. Though this is the only explicit reference to the return of Christ in the letter, the concept is implied often (1:28; 3:6,24). At the appearance both Christ and his followers would appear in glory. This picture differs somewhat from other Pauline pictures of the return, but moral impact rather than architectural consistency was the aim of such texts. On the glory of believers see Philippians 3:20f; 1 Corinthians 15:42ff; 2 Corinthians 5:1f; 1 John 3:2. On Christ as life see Philippians 1:21; Galatians 2:20; and 1 John 5:12.

IX. THINGS TO PUT TO DEATH (3:5-11)

[5]**Put to death, therefore, whatever belongs to your earthly nature: sexual immorality, impurity, lust, evil desires and greed, which is idolatry. **[6]**Because of these, the wrath of God is coming.**[a] [7]**You used to walk in these ways, in the life you once lived. **[8]**But now you must rid yourselves of all such things as these: anger, rage, malice, slander, and filthy language from your lips. **[9]**Do not lie to each other, since you**

---

[3]Bruce, *Epistles*, p. 135.

**have taken off your old self with its practices ¹⁰and have put
on the new self, which is being renewed in knowledge in the
image of its Creator. ¹¹Here there is no Greek or Jew, circumcised or uncircumcised, barbarian, Scythian, slave or
free, but Christ is all, and is in all.**

ᵃ6 Some early manuscripts *coming on those who are disobedient*

"Put to death" (νεκρώσατε, *nekrōsate*) is another uncompro-
mising imperative, as in verse 1, calling on the Christians to
grow in their faith (cf. 1:6). The two negative lists in this paragraph each contains five items, with an elaboration on the
fifth in each case. This grouping could reflect a custom of the
day with such lists, though it was not the style Paul always
used. These groupings may have assisted converts, instructed
at baptism, to remember. Of the many virtue and vice lists in
the New Testament, the ones most similar in form to this are
in Ephesians and 1 Peter. The sins condemned were all pagan
practices that Jews found particularly reprehensible.

**3:5 Put to death, therefore, whatever belongs to your earthly
nature:**
Understanding Christ, which Paul has promoted throughout the previous part of this letter, was to produce the lifestyle
which he will now set forth. This was no arbitrary list, giving
the terms of a bargain with God, but was a reflection of God's
nature as lived out by his people. Nor was it a compelled obedience, but a response of love to his love. "Put to death"
referred to a point of action from which their style of life was
to proceed. It also implied something of their lifestyles before
they became Christ's followers. The death idea reflects earlier
references in 2:11f, 20, and 3:3. "Earthly nature" (cf. the prohibition in 3:2) does not refer to anything characteristic of physical existence, but does refer to any immoral use of one's mind
and body. The Greek μέλη ... ἐπὶ τῆς γῆς (*melē...epi tēs gēs*), literally, is "members upon the earth," which the NIV interprets
as "earthly nature," changing a physical description to a spiritual — and properly so.

sexual immorality, impurity, lust, evil desires

The progress Paul has described has moved from knowledge ("set your hearts" in 3:1) to a disposition ("set your minds" in 3:2) to action ("put to death" here). The first four sins listed were sexual ones, which violated love for neighbor, and the fifth, greed, denied ultimate love for God. Sexual sins, in addition, violated the integrity of marriage and the family (cf. vv. 18-21). On sexual sins cf. Galatians 5:19; 1 Thessalonians 4:3; 1 Corinthians 5:6-11, 6:18f; Ephesians 5:5. "Sexual immorality" (πορνεία, *porneia*) refers to any unlawful sexual intercourse, though a primary application may have been to consorting with prostitutes. The Greek term is the root of the English "pornography." "Impurity" (ἀκαθαρσία, *akatharsia*) has the same general sense, but was a term of wider application (cf. Rom 1:24f). "Lust" or "passion" (πάθος, *pathos*) would be the evil desire leading to sexual immorality (cf. Rom 1:26; 1 Thess 4:5). The word in other contexts could refer to legitimate desire, as in 1 Timothy 3:1 ("desires" in the NIV). "Evil desires" (ἐπιθυμία, *epithymia*) also renders a word that could be used in the good sense, though obviously not here. The meaning here is close to that of the previous word. In Paul's lists it is not always possible to discern nuances of difference between the terms used. The overall impact was the thing.

and greed, which is idolatry.

"Greed" (πλεονεξία, *pleonexia*) is identified as "idolatry." It was seen as a rival religion, and thus was as dangerous in its way as was the heresy. Idolatry was abhorrent to the Jew, and the use of the term as a modifier here stresses the heinousness of a sin often glossed over and unrecognized. Greed is the inordinate desire for what one does not have. It may involve jealousy because of what others possess. It focuses on this life, and is self-centered. Thus it denies genuine love (contrast v. 14). Unfortunately it is often made to appear respectable. Even the Graeco-Roman world repudiated greed. In the New Testament see Luke 12:15; Romans 1:29; 1 Corinthians 5:10f;

6:10; and Ephesians 5:3. Lohse says greed seizes man's heart, leads him away from God, and imprisons him.[4]

3:6 Because of these, the wrath of God is coming.

This is Paul's first reference in Colossians to the negative side of God's final action (cf. Rom 1:18, 32; 1 Cor 5:13; 1 Thess 4:6). "Wrath" (ὀργή, *orgē*) is commonly seen as God's final judgment, and vice catalogues often ended with a statement like this. But it is also possible that the term referred to the very nature of God's universe, in which disobedience to God would finally bring judgment on itself, because it was not the way God's universe "works." This, of course, must also involve the final judgment, since often the wicked go through this life seeming to be happy and without mishap.

"Wrath" is seldom used by Paul to describe God. Weed suggests a better translation would be "disaster" — a term avoiding some of the negative implications associated with the other.[5] The language says that God, rich in mercy, must also be consistent with his nature. He could not act as if offenses to his very purity and being did not matter. If he did, what kind of a God would he be? The moral nature of the universe would be destroyed and chaos would result. "Wrath" does not show him a vindictive God eager to punish. It does show the seriousness of moral issues, and was a powerful motivator to turn to God. No one need experience God's wrath. One who failed to see its seriousness might treat morals lightly. Texts such as this warn against such unconcerned folly.

3:7 You used to walk in these ways, in the life you once lived.

This verse indicates that the Colossian church was largely Gentile, for the Jews found the behavior described in verse 6 abhorrent. Whereas other writings of Paul would stress the Holy Spirit as empowering the moral life, in Colossians it is

---

[4]Lohse, *Colossians*, p. 138.
[5]Weed, *Letters*, p. 85.

the relationship to Christ — death, burial and resurrection. The method and result in Christian experience were the same, but Paul spoke as he did here because of his stress on Christ throughout the epistle.

Translations which have the longer version of verse 6 ("those who are disobedient" — see the NIV footnote) translate the opening of this verse "among whom" rather than "these ways." The basic truth is not changed.

3:8 But now you must rid yourselves of all such things as these:

"Rid yourselves" is the image of putting off dirty or worn-out clothes. It may take its meaning from baptism, in which the candidate may have changed into some form of baptismal garment. Paul names five more vices, vices which could destroy social relations. As with the five in verse 6, here the last vice is elaborated. The first three were attitudinal, and the last two verbal. Of course they could interact in practice.

anger, rage, malice, slander, and filthy language from your lips.

"Anger" (ὀργή, orgē) and "rage" (θυμός, thymos) are very close in meaning, showing again that Paul aimed for total impact, rather than to distinguish between precise nuances. These attitudes would burst out in ways that would destroy relationships and deny love (v. 14). "Malice," a general term, may describe the attitude that would lead to slander and filthy language. "Slander" is, in the Greek, βλασφημία (blasphēmia, blasphemy). The New Testament usually has it describing speech against God or his servants. Here it probably had the broader idea of "abuse," which was a common usage in the world of that day (cf. Titus 3:5). "Filthy language" is from a word (αἰσχρολογία, aischrologia) found only here in the New Testament. Other translations render it "abusive" language, which perhaps catches the sense more accurately. It was not profanity in the commonly accepted sense. "Lying," in the next verse, was probably an illustration of Paul's meaning.

3:9 Do not lie to each other, since you have taken off your old self with its practices

Paul's emphases in these prohibitions would certainly be directed to his knowledge of the Colossian situation. Thus, lying would be a problem of the old life which may have crept into the church. So Paul says especially that they should not lie "to each other." The reference to taking off the old self is similar to "rid yourselves" of verse 8 and "putting off" of 2:11. It may also suggest the changing of clothes for baptism. Normally lying was associated with "filthy language" and perhaps with "slander" of the previous verse, but Pokorný suggests it sums the entire section from verse 3, since it was the opposite of preaching the truth, which was Christ.[6] Or was Paul attempting to associate lying with teaching heresy? That, however, seems strained, as does Pokorný's view.

3:10 and have put on the new self,

The reason to avoid lying (and all the other vices?) is continued here with the positive statement. The "new self" was not just personal change, but was the new human situation made possible through Christ. Christians, emerging from baptism, came into a new world. It was a world of new knowledge and new behavior. When the old behavior threatened to return, it was a world of discipline and prayer to overcome.

which is being renewed in knowledge in the image of its Creator.

"Renewed in knowledge" echoes Paul's prayer of 1:9ff (see also 2:3). The knowledge was more than cognition. This whole paranetic section indicates it was lifestyle. Knowledge, then, involved grasp of God's purpose and conformation to it. And it was to be a continuing process. The renewal was in the image of the Creator. This could be in God's image, indicating a return to God's original place for man (cf. Gen 1:26f). In view of 1:16, however, Paul may have had Christ in mind here. The result would be the same with either interpretation.

---

[6]Pokorný, *Colossians*, p. 168.

3:11 Here there is no Greek or Jew, circumcised or uncircumcised, barbarian, Scythian, slave or free, but Christ is all, and is in all.

This is a marvelous statement of the universal sweep of the gospel (cf. Gal 3:28; 1 Cor 12:13). But why did Paul put it here? If any rifts in the Colossian church had been along these lines, he has nowhere else indicated it. Could these be areas where "natural" animosities would likely lead to the kinds of mistreatment Paul had just condemned? Or was he amplifying the contrast of "old" and "new" of verses 9 and 10? Formerly there had been racial, religious, cultural and social barriers. They were now no longer relevant, for the new reality was either Christian or non-Christian. Love and proper treatment were to extend across that barrier. So in Christ the old sinful life and the old human divisions were done away. Christ was all, and in all. That relation was to govern everything!

"Greek" probably means all Greek-speaking Gentiles. Here they were mentioned before Jews, since Paul was writing to a Gentile church. Circumcision and uncircumcision refer to the literal act, not the spiritual act of 2:11. Barbarians were Gentiles who did not speak Greek. Scythians were at the low end of the barbarian scale. Josephus said they were little better than wild beasts, and in Attic comedy they were ridiculed as being uncouth in speech and action. Slave and free were categories on Paul's mind because of the situation with Onesimus, the runaway slave (4:9 and the book of Philemon). Though their societal status stayed the same, all enjoyed the same spiritual status.

X. THINGS TO PUT ON (3:12-17)

[12]**Therefore, as God's chosen people, holy and dearly loved, clothe yourselves with compassion, kindness, humility, gentleness and patience. [13]Bear with each other and forgive whatever grievances you may have against one another.**

Forgive as the Lord forgave you. [14]And over all these virtues put on love, which binds them all together in perfect unity.

[15]Let the peace of Christ rule in your hearts, since as members of one body you were called to peace. And be thankful. [16]Let the word of Christ dwell in you richly as you teach and admonish one another with all wisdom, and as you sing psalms, hymns and spiritual songs with gratitude in your hearts to God. [17]And whatever you do, whether in word or deed, do it all in the name of the Lord Jesus, giving thanks to God the Father through him.

3:12 Therefore, as God's chosen people, holy and dearly loved,

Paul now exhorts to positive characteristics, and lists five qualities, as he had previously given two lists of five vices each. "Therefore" grounds these exhortations in the "new world" created by God, and in all the powerful realities set forth throughout previous parts of this letter. These include God's choice of the Christians, a picture parallel to his choice of Israel. Christians were the new chosen race (cf. Rom 8:33; 1 Pet 2:9). "Holy" is the term found in 1:2,4 ("saints"). "Beloved" enhances the power of Paul's motivations.

clothe yourselves

Those who have rid themselves of vice now clothe themselves — again a possible reference to baptism. "Clothe" refers to a point of action, but obviously with continuing effects. The virtues noted were specific parts of the totally new way of thought and life. These qualities were to be present whether one was Greek, Jew, barbarian, Scythian, slave or free.

with compassion, kindness, humility, gentleness and patience.

"Compassion" (σπλάγχνα οἰκτιρμοῦ, *splanchna oiktirmou*) is literally "inward parts" (cf. Rom 12:1; 2 Cor 1:3 for *oiktirmos* by itself). It can mean the whole inner person. It was not just a virtue, but was a part of one's character. "Kindness" (χρησ-τότης, *chrēstotēs*) often describes God (cf. Rom 2:4; 1:22; Eph

2:7; Titus 3:4). God gave it to the totally undeserving, who were thus called to extend it to others, even to the undeserving. It was caring, the extending of blessings. "Humility" (ταπεινοφροσύνη, *tapeinophrosynē*) has been found in 2:18, 23, where the NIV translators have added "false" to indicate it was an undesirable trait in connection with the heresy. Here it was a virtue which was one quality that set Christians apart. In the Greek world at the time this quality was considered a weakness. "Gentleness" (πραΰτης, *prautēs*) involves considering others and even being willing to give up one's rights to help them (cf. 2 Cor 10:11; Gal 5:23, 6:1; Eph 4:2). Some translations render the word "meekness," which implies self-control and avoidance of excessive self-concern. "Patience" (μακροθυμία, *makrothymia*, cf. Rom 2:4; 9:22) endures wrong and puts up with the frustration produced by others without becoming unduly and unwisely irritated. Cf. "bear with" in the next verse.

3:13 Bear with each other and forgive whatever grievances you may have against one another. Forgive as the Lord forgave you.

Bearing and forgiveness were functions of the attitudes specified in verse 12. The call to forgive echoes Jesus' teaching (see Matt 18:23; Luke 11:3) but draws further significance from his death and resurrection. The word χαρίζομαι (*charizomai*, "grant forgiveness") translated "forgive" and "forgave" is not the usual New Testament term, but stresses the grace (unmerited blessing) involved in Christ's sacrifice. See also Romans 8:32; 1 Corinthians 2:12; Galatians 3:18; Ephesians 4:32; Philippians 1:29, 2:9; and Colossians 2:13. "Grievances" suggests the idea of unremitted debts, and may indicate the presence of such feeling in the congregation. The aggrieved person was to take the initiative, as God took the initiative for man's sake. Did Paul have in mind any attitude toward the heretics, hoping that gracious overtures would lead them to repentance? We cannot say. It is clear here and throughout that forgiving was more than just a command given to Christians. It was woven into the very fabric of God's action in Christ. To refuse it would be to deny the very nature of Christianity.

3:14 And over all these virtues put on love, which binds them all together in perfect unity.

Paul spoke of the supremacy of love in 1 Corinthians 13:1-3, and said all other commandments were summed up in love in Romans 13:9f. Here he elevates it above the virtues he had enumerated, as that which bound them in perfect unity. There are two views of his meaning. One is that love, like a belt, holds the other virtues together. The idea may be that if one is loving then the other virtues would be a part of that love. This would seem to agree with 1 Corinthians 13:1-3 and Romans 13:9f. The other view is that love binds the members of the church together so that they are led to perfect unity. Love would solve all problems of division among Christians. In either event the profound importance of love must be affirmed.

3:15 Let the peace of Christ rule in your hearts, since as members of one body you were called to peace.

Those who love one another are at peace. On the peace of Christ cf. John 14:27; Ephesians 2:14; Philippians 4:7 and 2 Thessalonians 3:16. This was peace in community, not simply inner peace. "Rule" indicates control. Their relationships should be controlled by peace.

And be thankful.

"Thankful" (εὐχάριστος, *eucharistos*) picks up Paul's words in 1:12. The particular focus here would be gratitude for the forgiveness and new life from God described in the previous verse. This was intrinsic to the faith, and was to be the Christian's constant motivation.

3:16 Let the word of Christ dwell in you richly

Paul instructs his readers to love each other (v. 14), to be at peace with each other (v. 15), and now to teach and admonish each other. This verse is a lovely picture of a harmonious community at worship. Teaching and admonishing had their ground in the Word of Christ. This was probably the message about Christ (see 1:15-20) and thus the message about redemption. One might also think of the teachings of Christ, but they do not seem to be the focus of this letter.

"In you" could be a personal indwelling, or could mean within the community. Throughout the epistle this word about Christ has been Paul's constant antidote to the heretical teaching. When the church was centered in that message, false doctrine could not gain a foothold.

as you teach and admonish one another with all wisdom,

Teaching and admonition are activities of those who love one another, and who wish to help others grow in Christ. No view of the corporate activities of Christians can afford to neglect this. "Wisdom" could modify teaching and admonishing, as in the NIV, or it could modify "sing." The term would imply acting judiciously and in a manner that would be most effective. It can be understood as a call to the church to carefully examine and select its hymns so that they would be used wisely. On wisdom in Colossians see 1:9,28; 2:3,23; and 4:5.

The parallel to this text is Ephesians 5:19, which says "speak to one another." Although we cannot be certain, perhaps the early church employed antiphonal singing. There is a question as to whether the singing was the vehicle of teaching or whether it was a separate activity. We consider it to be the former, on the basis of the parallel with Ephesians 5:19. In addition to 1:15-20, other New Testament texts considered to be early Christian hymns are Philippians 2:5-11; Ephesians 5:14; 1 Timothy 3:16 and 2 Timothy 2:11-13.

and as you sing psalms, hymns and spiritual songs

Scholars agree it is virtually impossible to make nice distinctions between psalms, hymns, and spiritual songs. "Psalms" is used, of course, of Old Testament psalms. The basic meaning is a song of praise. The Christians probably composed new songs of praise, modelled on the Old Testament psalms, appropriate to their faith in Christ (cf. 1 Cor 14:26). The verbal form of the word is found in 1 Corinthians 14:15 and James 5:13. "Hymns" (a transliteration of the Greek ὕμνος, *hymnos*) is also a term describing songs of praise. The only other New Testament usage is Ephesians 5:19, but the related verb form is found in Mark 14:26 and parallels, and in Acts 16:25. "Songs" (ᾠδή, *ōdē*) is also a song praising God's acts, as in Revelation 5:9; 14:3; and 15:3. None of these terms implies anything about the activity itself beyond the actual singing.

"Spiritual" (πνευματικός, *pneumatikos*) may modify all three terms. Some consider this as Spirit-prompted singing. Others think it refers to the content of the songs, or to the gratitude to God which prompted the singing of them. Since Colossians says so little about the Holy Spirit, we incline to the latter view.

with gratitude in your hearts to God.

"Gratitude" translates the word χάρις (charis) usually rendered "grace." Since the term is used with the definite article, and since Paul was not speaking of the aesthetic value of the singing, but of its teaching role, "gratitude" seems an appropriate translation. It also parallels the references to thankfulness in verses 15 and 17.

3:17 And whatever you do, whether in word or deed,

In a sense this verse climaxes the main paranetic section of Colossians and sums up what Paul had been saying. It is appropriate that such a statement climax the depiction of Christ Paul has been making throughout. Next Paul will give the household rules (3:18–4:1) which stand as a separate unit. This will be followed by a personal request (4:2-4), a brief exhortation (4:5,6) and closing greetings and instructions (4:7-18).

do it all in the name of the Lord Jesus, giving thanks to God the Father through him.

This universal statement directed readers in a life perspective. Those who pursued it did not need to be given specific

rules for every possible circumstance. "In the name" can indicate all Jesus was, all he taught, and the acknowledgment of his
role as savior. "Thanks" (cf. 1:12; 3:15) could be an additional
note, but we think it more likely the words and deeds were to
be spurred by gratitude for Christ's love. The whole expression
may be drawn from the baptismal procedure, as has so much
of the language of the preceding verses (cf. Rom 10:9, 13;
1 Cor 1:2,10,31; Eph 4:5; 5:20; 1 Thess 1:12; 3:6; 2 Tim 2:19;
1 John 2:12; 3:23; 5:13). Baptism has been central in Paul's
thought throughout as he has penned this letter, since it was a
decisive act in an individual's commitment to Christ.

XI. RULES FOR THE CHRISTIAN HOUSEHOLD
(3:18–4:1)

A. HUSBANDS AND WIVES (3:18-19)

[18]**Wives, submit to your husbands, as is fitting in the
Lord.**
[19]**Husbands, love your wives and do not be harsh with
them.**

This section and others like it in the New Testament have
been called "house tables," or "rules for the household." See
similar material in Ephesians 5:22–6:9; 1 Timothy 2:8-15; 6:1f;
Titus 2:1-10; 1 Peter 2:18–3:7; and outside the New Testament
in Didache 4:9-11; Epistle of Barnabas 19:5-7; First Clement
1:3; 2:6-9; Ignatius to Polycarp 4:1–6:2; and Polycarp to the
Philippians 4:2–6:1. The different style of this material is obvious even to the casual reader. The relationships occur in
pairs, with the subordinate member listed first, and the relations move from the closest to the most remote. It was generally assumed that Christians would obey the exhortations to
both parties, so that there was a symbiotic relationship. Paul
does not say here, for example, what the Christian wife of a
non-Christian husband ought to do if he mistreated her. Here
her submission is met by his love, and vice versa.

The normal form of these admonitions first lists the member addressed, then gives the imperative, and finally (usually) gives a motivation. Some of these same instructions could be found in non-Christian ethical instructions, but in them the motivation would differ. Note how often these verses refer to the Lord (Master) — 18,20,22,23,24 (twice) and 4:1. These relations give specific form to "all in the name of the Lord Jesus" of verse 17.

There has been much discussion, but no consensus, about the origin of these housetables. Were they adapted and modified by Christians from some non-Christian background? That sort of adaptation was done by Hellenistic Jews in their synagogues. If so, what was the background? Might they have been part of the instruction given new converts before or following baptism? If so, it seems strange that certain New Testament books (Romans, 1 Corinthians, 1, 2 Thessalonians, James, and John's writings) omit them. It does seem significant, though, that these instructions take similar form in various New Testament writings, implying they may have been somewhat "fixed" in many churches. The questions posed here have still not been answered definitively.

Were these standards only relevant to the cultural situation of the day, or were they of eternal validity? Often personal agendas determine how individuals answer this question. If one takes all Paul's writings into account, it is clear he had a hierarchical view of relationships, especially husband and wife (see 1 Cor 11:3,7-9; Eph 5:23ff). He placed his instructions in the context of relation to the Lord (see 1 Cor 11:2-16 and Eph 5:22-33). He also said in Christ there was neither male nor female (Gal 3:28) which, though indicating equal access to salvation, no more abrogates the nature of that interrelationship than it says slaves were no longer slaves. If one begins to eliminate Paul's words on a cultural basis, it would be difficult to know where to stop the process. Further the rightness or wrongness of a matter cannot be determined by whether or not it was culturally "correct." Behind such an argument is the supposition that the view of culture held by the person making the argument is the correct one.

Since much of a person's life was lived in the household, it was important that Christianity offer instructions aimed directly at those relationships.

3:18 Wives, submit to your husbands, as is fitting in the Lord.

The wife's submission is here treated as a status she chose because of her relation to the Lord. "Submit" (ὑποτάσσεσθε, *hupotassesthe*) in Greek is in middle voice, i.e., "submit your-self" — choose to do so. Paul's words give no comfort to the chauvinist, since "love" in the following verse tempers and conditions submission. It would be no burden to submit to love. The same complementary relationship between love and submission is seen in Ephesians 5:22-33, and in 1 Corinthians 7:3f, Paul also speaks of the "rights" of both partners. Thus nothing demeaning to the wife can be deduced from Paul's language here. Nor is there any indication of a natural inferiority of the wife to her husband. After all everyone must submit to someone, if only to God.

3:19 Husbands, love your wives

The counterpoint to the submission of the wife is the love of the husband. "Love" translates the term found in verse 14, and is the same word (*agapē*) the New Testament uses of God's love for man. This word was not found in any secular list of household duties. No motivation clause is found here because love in Christian terms carried its motivation within itself; love was "absolutely valid."[7]

and do not be harsh with them.

The prohibition of harshness is literally "don't be embittered" (μὴ πικραίνεσθε, *mē pikrainesthe*). This would call for patience with faults, and also for a refusal to vent on the wife bitterness generated by outside circumstances. Weed points out that Paul's words are in contrast to Jewish and

---

[7]Lohse, *Colossians*, p. 158.

pagan ethics which gave husbands all the rights and wives all the duties.[8]

B. CHILDREN AND FATHERS (3:20-21)

[20]**Children, obey your parents in everything, for this pleases the Lord.**

[21]**Fathers, do not embitter your children, or they will become discouraged.**

3:20 Children, obey your parents in everything, for this pleases the Lord.

Children are addressed as being responsible, contrary to pagan ethics. Further they are asked to obey, rather than the fathers being asked to enforce obedience. "Obey" (ὑπακούω, *hypakouō*) is a stronger term than "submit" in verse 18, and "everything" adds further strength. We are not told if the children had become Christians, but as part of a Christian household they were to respect its rules. The verse ends, in Greek, with "in the Lord," probably meaning "in the Christian sphere." The Jewish background for these words is found in Exodus 20:12 and Deuteronomy 5:16. Again it is assumed the fathers act as Christians should (v. 21, Eph 6:4). Paul does not discuss cases of unreasonable parents or rebellious children.

3:21 Fathers, do not embitter your children, or they will become discouraged.

We presume fathers are addressed because of their special responsibility, but one would suppose these instructions would apply to both parents, since verse 20 indicates obedience to both parents. In the Roman culture the father's parental authority was unlimited, so that this teaching would considerably temper any extremes. As O'Brien says, the idea here is

---

[8]Weed, *Letter*, p. 94.

responsibility to children, not authority over them.[9] The word translated "embittered" (from ἐρεθίζω, *erethizo*) is found elsewhere in the New Testament in 2 Corinthians 9:2 ("stirred," NIV). Some translations have "provoke" here. The word may refer to nagging or belittling of the children. If they were constantly criticized, they might feel it was impossible to become worthwhile persons. A sense of failure inbred into children could poison their entire lifetimes. The opposite term from "discouraged" (ἀθυμέω, *athymeo*) means "take heart," and refers to the "undergirding presence of God" in Acts 27:22,25 and 36.[10]

C. SLAVES AND MASTERS (3:22–4:1)

[22]Slaves, obey your earthly masters in everything; and do it, not only when their eye is on you and to win their favor, but with sincerity of heart and reverence for the Lord. [23]Whatever you do, work at it with all your heart, as working for the Lord, not for men, [24]since you know that you will receive an inheritance from the Lord as a reward. It is the Lord Christ you are serving. [25]Anyone who does wrong will be repaid for his wrong, and there is no favoritism.

[1]Masters, provide your slaves with what is right and fair, because you know that you also have a Master in heaven.

3:22 Slaves, obey your earthly masters in everything;

The instructions to slaves are as lengthy as those to all other groups combined. This may indicate a large number of slaves in the church, or that problems with slaves were a particularly challenging case for Christian ethics. The case of Onesimus was on Paul's mind, and though the issues discussed in Philemon are not those noted here, they may have been relevant to Onesimus before his escape (cf. the book of

---

[9]O'Brien, *Colossians*, pp. 225f.
[10]Pokorný, *Colossians*, p. 182.

Philemon). We are given an interesting look at the attitudes of some slaves. Paul's words indicate a radical change of heart from what was otherwise the case in society.

and do it, not only when their eye is on you and to win their favor, but with sincerity of heart and reverence for the Lord.

"Earthly masters" is a reminder that the slave owner's sovereignty over his slaves was not absolute. There was a higher authority governing the relationship. "Obey in everything" is the same language as that used in verse 20. "Their eye is upon you" could imply they would work only when watched, or that they were trying to attract attention. The Greek is literally "eye service" (ὀφθαλμοδουλία, *ophthalmodoulia*), and the first known usages are here and in Ephesians 6:6. "Sincerity" indicates undivided loyalty (the NRSV has "wholeheartedly"). What higher motivation could be given than "reverence for the Lord" (literally, "fearing")? In a sense, then, a slave's daily service was worship.

3:23 Whatever you do, work at it with all your heart, as working for the Lord, not for men,

This verse is similar to verse 17. A slave who worked as "for the Lord" need never suffer anxiety over failure to serve his owner (assuming the owner were reasonable, and not a tyrant.) "Working for the Lord" expands on "reverence for the Lord."

3:24 since you know that you will receive an inheritance from the Lord as a reward. It is the Lord Christ you are serving.

This verse strengthens the motivation of the slave. For the third consecutive verse relation to the Lord is noted. Under Roman law slaves could not inherit, so Paul's "inheritance" would be a particularly striking statement. Not only inheritance, but what an inheritance (cf. 1:5,12,27; 3:1-4)! The word translated "reward" (ἀνταπόδοσις, *antapodosis*) is only here in the New Testament. "Serving" could also be translated as an imperative;

i.e., "you serve." The word δουλεύω (*douleuō*) is the verbal form of the usual word for slave (*doulos*). They were, finally, slaves of Christ, which determined their earthly demeanor.

In the other relationships of verses 18-21 a reciprocity is supposed. Here the case may be different. Ought not the slave to obey, whatever the treatment given by the master? 1 Peter 2:18ff indicates they should.

It is also intriguing to imagine the situation in the church if a slave was an overseer/elder. Then in that sphere he would be concerned, as a shepherd, for the spiritual health of his Christian master. Yet in everyday life he would still have the obligation Paul describes here. This could be a delicate situation for both slave and master.

3:25 Anyone who does wrong will be repaid for his wrong, and there is no favoritism.

This is the other side of the inheritance pictured in verse 24. The principle stated was universal and inescapable (cf. Gal 6:7f). Though in the broader sense all were under this principle, the question here is whether Paul spoke to slaves, to masters, or to both. Those who think it was slaves point out that masters are not specifically addressed till the next verse, and that the word for "do wrong" (ἀδικέω, *adikeō*, "act unjustly") is used of Onesimus in Philemon 18. On the other hand are those who say masters could wrong their slaves, but not vice versa. Those arguing for masters note that the word translated "favoritism" is applied to masters in Ephesians 6:9.

Whatever the primary sense, neither group would receive special consideration. If there were "favoritism" in this life, there would be none in God's judgment. Those who treated others wrongly should fear, and those wrongly treated should take heart.

4:1 Masters, provide your slaves with what is right and fair, because you know that you also have a Master in heaven.

The implication of "earthly masters" in 3:22 is now made specific. Christian masters were themselves slaves under the heavenly master, and were called upon to serve the Lord as their slaves were to serve them. Though slavery in the first Christian century is often pictured as harsh and repressing, both pagan and Jewish moralists laid down principles for humane treatment. Thus "right" and "fair" would be understood even outside Christian circles. The difference with Christians was the motivation.

Christianity, at this point, was not fomenting major social revolution. Slavery was accepted as a given. It has been said that when Christian principles were thoroughly understood and accepted in society, slavery became more difficult, and eventually impossible.

Christians may ask if these principles apply to the relation of employer and employee. Though the question has difficult nuances, it is hard to see how either a Christian employer or employee could ignore the mandates given here, since they are anchored in a relation with the Lord.

COLOSSIANS 4

XII. FINAL EXHORTATIONS TO PRAYER AND PROPER BEHAVIOR (4:2-6)

²Devote yourselves to prayer, being watchful and thankful. ³And pray for us, too, that God may open a door for our message, so that we may proclaim the mystery of Christ, for which I am in chains. ⁴Pray that I may proclaim it clearly, as I should. ⁵Be wise in the way you act toward outsiders; make the most of every opportunity. ⁶Let your conversation be always full of grace, seasoned with salt, so that you may know how to answer everyone.

Paul moves, in verses 2-4, from the Colossians' needs to his own needs. Then with a brief exhortation (vv. 5, 6) he moves into his closing remarks (vv. 7ff). Cf. Paul's other requests for intercession in Romans 15:30-32; 2 Corinthians 1:11; Ephesians 6:19; Philippians 1:19; 1 Thessalonians 5:25; 2 Thessalonians 3:1f; and Philemon 22.

4:2 Devote yourselves to prayer, being watchful and thankful.
Paul calls his readers to a committed prayer life, just as he began the letter in prayer for them (1:3). Though this verse is general, Paul probably had in mind the specific requests of the next two verses. Melick points out that the last half of the verse is literally "be watchful in thankfulness," and criticizes the NIV for being too general in its translation.[1] Some argue "being watchful" (from γρηγορέω, *grēgoreō*) indicates expecta-

---

[1]Melick, *Colossians*, p. 241.

tion of the Second Coming, since the term was often used in that connection. We think, rather, that it indicated a prayer life that was active and alert. Jesus so instructed his followers in Matthew 24:42f; 25:13; and Luke 18:8, and Paul admonished Christians to be alert (1 Thessalonians 5:6; 1 Corinthians 16:13). Paul was modifying prayer with "watchful" and "thankful" rather than offering separate commands.

The idea of thanks is found here for the seventh time in Colossians (1:2,12; 2:2,7; 3:15,16,17).

4:3 And pray for us, too, that God may open a door for our message, so that we may proclaim the mystery of Christ, for which I am in chains.

Paul's "us" included his companions, to be named subsequently, in his request. In the next verse he reverts to the singular. Paul was able to preach, even while a prisoner. Onesimus was converted (Phlm 10), and the palace guard knew he was in chains for Christ (Phil 1:13; and cf. Acts 28:30f) Paul would obviously wish to be freed, and the "open door" might imply that. But even more important to him were opportunities for evangelism. He was convinced that through the work of God significant opportunities could be made available — a lesson for the church in all ages! On the open door cf. 1 Corinthians 16:9; 2 Corinthians 2:12; and Acts 14:27.

4:4 Pray that I may proclaim it clearly, as I should.

"Proclaim" (φανερόω, *phaneroō*) or "reveal" (NRSV) is a word normally used to refer to divine revelation. This is the only place Paul used it to describe his preaching. "Clearly" may mean with clarity, so that he wanted God's message to be plainly and effectively spoken for what it was — from God and not from man. Others suggest "clearly" may have been a request for skill in his defense, or for ability to refute the heresy effectively. We consider these last two less likely.

"As I should" translates a word that often indicates a sense of divine compulsion — "it is necessary" (δεῖ, *dei*).

4:5 Be wise in the way you act toward outsiders;

Paul now gives instructions in another relationship (cf. 3:18–4:1) — Christians toward outsiders (non-Christians). Note similar language in Ephesians 5:15f. The call for wisdom catches up the theme of 1:9,28; 2:3 and 3:16, but here it has a different thrust — certainly practical and probably evangelistic. Other texts dealing with relations to outsiders are 1 Corinthians 10:32f; Philippians 2:14f; 1 Thessalonians 4:11f; 1 Timothy 3:7; 6:1; Titus 2:8; and 1 Peter 2:15; 3:1,16. Wise behavior involved constructive use of situations (boldness?) and speaking with tact and judiciousness.

make the most of every opportunity.

The Greek for "make the most" (from ἐξαγοράζω, *exagorazō*) is translated by O'Brien "snapping up every opportunity."[2] There is a sense of urgency here, though that didn't necessarily mean Paul had an imminent parousia in mind. Christians ought always to feel a similar urgency (exercised with good sense) to draw people to the Lord. Time and opportunity should not be wasted.

4:6 Let your conversation be always full of grace, seasoned with salt, so that you may know how to answer everyone.

From actions (v. 5) Paul now moves to words. "Grace" (χάρις, *charis*) suggests the entire Christian experience, which only is possible through grace. One theory of the meaning of the term here is that it means gracious or charming speech which would overcome suspicion and win a favorable hearing. Another view considers it speech that was characterized by gratitude. A third position holds that it meant preaching the message of grace, i. e., the gospel. The following image, of salt, may augment the idea of gracious or charming speech. In rabbinic thought salt could indicate wisdom. It could also flavor, making the dish to which it was applied more attractive and enjoyable. Perhaps Paul was saying that words should

---

[2]O'Brien, *Colossians*, p. 241.

be used so as to gain the greatest favor for Christians and their message. On salt see Matthew 5:13; Mark 9:50; and Luke 14:34. On "answer" see 1 Peter 3:15f.

XIII. FINAL INSTRUCTIONS AND GREETINGS (4:7-18)

A. TYCHICUS AND ONESIMUS (4:7-9)

[7]Tychicus will tell you all the news about me. He is a dear brother, a faithful minister and fellow servant in the Lord. [8]I am sending him to you for the express purpose that you may know about our[a] circumstances and that he may encourage your hearts. [9]He is coming with Onesimus, our faithful and dear brother, who is one of you. They will tell you everything that is happening here.

[a]*8* Some manuscripts *that he may know about your*

The last section of this letter speaks first of the two messengers Paul was sending (vv. 7-9). Then he sends greetings from six of his companions (vv. 10-14). Paul himself sent greetings, along with special instructions for the church and for Archippus (vv. 15-17), before the closing address. Save for Tychicus and Nympha, and perhaps Jesus Justus, all the names in these verses are also mentioned in Philemon. It is a long list for a church Paul had never visited. Most names are accompanied by a lengthy description of the person.

4:7 Tychicus will tell you all the news about me.

Paul avoids personal references in these closing verses, since Tychicus would convey that information. But writing the rest of the letter himself insured his thoughts would be carried exactly, and that they would be read to the church just as he wrote them (v. 16). In other letters Paul has given more personal information (Galatians, Philippians, 2 Corinthians) but he did so either to teach or as a defense of himself or his message.

Letter carrying in Paul's day was a chancy business. Tychicus was from Asia (Acts 20:4) and was once sent by Paul to Crete (Titus 3:12) and to Ephesus (2 Tim 4:12). Since the wording of Ephesians 6:21f is very similar to the present text, it is thought Tychicus may have carried Ephesians (an earlier trip than that noted in 2 Tim 4:12) to Ephesus, and, if it was a circular letter, to other churches in Asia Minor as well. Here he may also have carried the letter to Philemon and one to the church at Laodicea. He was accompanied on his trip by Onesimus (v. 9).

He is a dear brother, a faithful minister and fellow servant in the Lord.

Tychicus is called a "dear brother," as was Onesimus in verse nine, and "fellow servant" as was Epaphras (1:7; cf. 4:12). In the latter case the term may have been used to encourage giving Tychicus the same reception as they might give Epaphras, whom they knew well.

4:8 I am sending him to you for the express purpose that you may know about our circumstances and that he may encourage your hearts.

Paul thrice indicates Tychicus would give news about him (vv. 7,8,9). Was Paul encouraging the Colossians to press Tychicus for personal information? The additional note here refers to Tychicus as an encourager.

4:9 He is coming with Onesimus, our faithful and dear brother, who is one of you. They will tell you everything that is happening here.

Onesimus was surely the converted runaway slave of Philemon. Nothing is said about the problem discussed in Philemon, but just that he was a "faithful and dear brother" — the language used of Tychicus and Epaphras. He was also "one of them," i.e., from Colosse. The implication is that to them he was a Christian and was to be received as such, whatever the nature of his relationship with Philemon. No doubt his acceptance by the church would be an encouragement to Philemon to receive him back in love, as Paul requested in his letter to Philemon. The case of Onesimus and Philemon would be a chance to implement the master-slave aspect of the household rules mentioned in 3:22–4:1.

B. GREETINGS (4:10-15)

[10]My fellow prisoner Aristarchus sends you his greetings, as does Mark, the cousin of Barnabas. (You have received instructions about him; if he comes to you, welcome him.) [11]Jesus, who is called Justus, also sends greetings. These are the only Jews among my fellow workers for the kingdom of God, and they have proved a comfort to me. [12]Epaphras, who is one of you and a servant of Christ Jesus, sends greetings. He is always wrestling in prayer for you, that you may stand firm in all the will of God, mature and fully assured. [13]I vouch for him that he is working hard for you and for those at Laodicea and Hierapolis. [14]Our dear friend Luke, the doctor, and Demas send greetings. [15]Give my greetings to the brothers at Laodicea, and to Nympha and the church in her house.

4:10 My fellow prisoner Aristarchus sends you his greetings,

Of the six greetings in this paragraph three were Gentiles and three Jews. Aristarchus was from Thessalonica (Acts 20:4), had been with Paul during the riot in Ephesus (Acts 19:29), and was on the ship which began carrying Paul to Rome and thus probably on the next vessel Paul rode, which was wrecked. He may have been constantly with Paul in Rome since then. "Fellow prisoner" may indicate incarceration, or may mean he was Christ's slave, as was Paul. Epaphras, in verse 12, is not called a prisoner here, though he was so designated in Philemon 23. This has led to the novel suggestion that Paul's friends may have voluntarily shared his imprisonment on a rotating basis (Aristarchus now, Epaphras another time). Aristarchus also sent greetings to Philemon (Phlm 24). Tradition says he was martyred at Rome under Nero.

as does Mark, the cousin of Barnabas.

Mark was no doubt John Mark, Paul's former companion who had turned back on the southern coast of Asia Minor. He was subsequently the subject of a disagreement between Paul and Barnabas (Acts 12:12,25; 13:13; 15:36-41). Paul may have once had negative feelings toward Mark, or may simply have concluded some people, Mark included, were not cut out for extended mission trips. At any rate according to this text and to Philemon 24, he was with Paul. In 2 Timothy 4:12 Paul asked that Timothy bring Mark along to join him where he was imprisoned (cf. also 1 Peter 5:13). In the present text Paul notes the possibility Mark might go to Colosse. Perhaps he could have accompanied Tychicus and Onesimus.

This is the only text where Barnabas and Mark are identified as cousins. Mark had gone with Barnabas on missionary work to Cyprus (Acts 15:39) and since Barnabas was famous as an exhorter and a peacemaker (Acts 9:27; 11:22-26) he may have helped stabilize Mark and make of him a more effective minister. The reference to Barnabas indicates he was known to the Colossian church.

(You have received instructions about him; if he comes to you, welcome him.)

We do not know who sent the "instructions" about Mark, but Paul seems the most likely possibility. Nor do we know of what they consisted. "Welcome" (from δέχομαι, *dechomai*) is a term requesting the best sort of reception.

4:11 Jesus, who is called Justus, also sends greetings. These are the only Jews among my fellow workers for the kingdom of God, and they have proved a comfort to me.

Jesus Justus is otherwise unknown. If Philemon 23 is read

with a comma between "Christ" and "Jesus" he was also noted there. Otherwise not (as in the NIV). Does "only Jews" mean the only Jews with Paul in Rome? It is hard to think they would be the only ones anywhere. This could show how the complexion of the church was taking a more Gentile coloring. Is there a note of pathos in Paul's words? "Kingdom of God" is used in the present sense (cf. 1:13). Acts 28:30f speaks of Paul preaching the kingdom of God "totally and without hindrance" while he was imprisoned. "Comfort" (παρηγορία, *parēgoria*) is a strong term, the root for the English "paregoric."

4:12 Epaphras, who is one of you and a servant of Christ Jesus, sends greetings. He is always wrestling in prayer for you, that you may stand firm in all the will of God, mature and fully assured.

Epaphras (1:7) may have been sent to evangelize Colosse while Paul was in Ephesus on his third journey. He was a Colossian native. Some think he had gone to visit Paul in Rome to inquire about dealing with the heresy, which he no doubt understood better than anyone. The language in which Paul describes him is the same Paul used of himself and Timothy. His prayer concerns echo those of Paul in 1:28f; 2:1f; and cf. 1:23; 2:7. "Wrestling" is from the Greek term ἀγωνίζομαι (*agōnizomai*) at the root of the English "agonizing." The same root is found in 1:29 and 2:1. "Mature and fully assured" may have been said with special reference to the heresy. The term πληροφορέω (*plērophoreō*), translated "fully assured," could also be rendered "filled," which could reflect Paul's words about fullness being found only in Christ (2:10).

4:13 I vouch for him that he is working hard for you and for those at Laodicea and Hierapolis.

Epaphras had a multichurch ministry. On the church in Laodicea see verse 16 and Revelation 3:1-7. Paul did not give further definition to "working hard."

4:14 Our dear friend Luke, the doctor,

This is one of only three New Testament references to

Luke (Phlm 23, 2 Tim 4:11) and is the only place where he was called a doctor. Why was his profession noted here? Did he give Paul medical attention? Luke is considered a Gentile on the basis of this listing with Gentiles. Earle Ellis, however, argues that Luke was a Hellenistic Jew. As the author of Luke and Acts, Luke actually authored the largest portion of the New Testament.

and Demas send greetings.

Demas is also mentioned in Philemon 24, where, sadly, he passes from our sight as one who "loved this world" and had deserted Paul (2 Tim 4:10).

4:15 Give my greetings to the brothers at Laodicea,

A possible reason greetings were extended to Laodicea and not to Hierapolis could be because Laodicea was on the road to Colosse, and Hierapolis was not. Hence a Christian traveller going to Colosse could easily convey word to Laodicea on the way. A letter was sent to the church in Laodicea (v. 16), possibly by Paul. These additional greetings may have been to enhance relations between the churches, or perhaps because Paul knew there would be frequent travel between the cities.

and to Nympha and the church in her house.

Variant readings make it unclear whether Nympha was a man or a woman. The modifying pronoun reads "her," "his," and even "their," depending on which manuscript is read. Bruce argues it was a woman since no scribe would have changed a male name to a female.[3] House churches often are mentioned in the New Testament (Acts 16:15,40; Rom 16:23; 1 Cor 16:19). The early Christians had no buildings. House churches may have been small congregations, or perhaps subgroups of a larger congregation that assembled in some larger facility. A church also met in the house of Philemon (Phlm 2).

---

[3]Bruce, *Epistles*, p. 183.

C. CONCLUDING INSTRUCTIONS (4:16-18)

[16]After this letter has been read to you, see that it is also read in the church of the Laodiceans and that you in turn read the letter from Laodicea. [17]Tell Archippus: "See to it that you complete the work you have received in the Lord." [18]I, Paul, write this greeting in my own hand. Remember my chains. Grace be with you.

4:16 After this letter has been read to you, see that it is also read in the church of the Laodiceans

Paul's instructions to read the letter in Laodicea may indicate the heresy was a threat there as well. It indicates that letters were read aloud in the assembly (1 Thess 5:27), as were the Old Testament Scriptures (cf. 1 Tim 4:13), perhaps indicating they were considered as equal in authority to the Old Testament. If the letters were not, the message of Christ was. We can see, as well, why Paul's letters would be copied and sent out (cf. 2 Pet 3:15f).

and that you in turn read the letter from Laodicea.

The "letter from Laodicea" has been much discussed. Early opinions held that it was sent from Paul to Laodicea, and then was to be sent from there to Colosse. Later opinion thinks it to be from the church in Laodicea. How would Paul know of it then? Did he assume they would reply to the reading of Colossians in the church there?

Attempts have been made, inconclusively, to identify this letter with Ephesians or Philemon.[4] Since it fits no New Testament epistle it is presumed to be lost, as was some Corinthian correspondence (1 Cor 5:9; 2 Cor 2:4). This gap led to a later fabricated "letter of Paul to the Laodiceans."

---

[4]See the discussion in O'Brien, *Colossians*, pp. 257f. For support of the Ephesian position, see Kenneth Boles, *Galatians and Ephesians*, p. 182.

4:17 Tell Archippus: "See to it that you complete the work you have received in the Lord."

Archippus is mentioned in Philemon 2 and may have been the son of Philemon and Apphia. He is there called a "fellow soldier." We know neither his task nor why this public encouragement was given. It may have had something to do with Onesimus. But this is unlikely, since that would depend on his having received the letter to Philemon. Perhaps the task dealt with the refutation of the heresy. In that case the public encouragement might have been to impress him with the seriousness of the charge. It is not necessary to assume a criticism. Some suggest he may have lived in Laodicea and had special responsibilities there. The term for "work" (δια–κονία, *diakonia*) is from the same root as "deacon." There is no indication in this case that it was an office in the church (cf. 1 Tim 3:8ff).

4:18 I, Paul, write this greeting in my own hand. Remember my chains. Grace be with you.

As Paul often did, he closed by putting his own hand on the pen (cf. 1 Cor 16:21; 2 Cor 10:1; Gal 6:11; 2 Thess 3:17; Phlm 19). It was a common custom, after the scribe's work, for the author to append a personal close. The letter opened by joining Timothy's name with Paul, but this indicates Paul alone was the author. "Chains" is a final reminder of the power of the gospel to capture a life, even though imprisonment could result. Let their prayer continue ("remember"). Paul closes, as he began, by bestowing grace upon his readers.

THE BOOK OF
PHILEMON

INTRODUCTION

This shortest of Paul's letters is similar to private correspondence of the day, but takes on a broader importance because of its skillful application of Christian principles and its inclusion in the canon. The correspondences with Colossians prompt the conclusion that it was sent at the same time as that letter, by the hand of Tychicus, who was accompanied by Onesimus. Both of these messengers were part of the church at Colosse (Col 4:9,17), so it is assumed that Philemon was also.

Onesimus, a slave, had run away from Philemon, his master, and fled to Rome (assuming that was the place of Paul's imprisonment — see the introduction to Colossians). There he somehow came into contact with the apostle, and became a follower of Jesus. Paul now faced a dilemma with both legal and Christian implications. In the latter instance he was bound to inform Philemon, his friend and Christian brother, of the situation, and to send Onesimus home. But suppose Philemon would not receive his returned slave charitably? It seems Onesimus had done wrong and thus was under obligation to Philemon (v. 18). It is also possible that Paul wished Philemon to send Onesimus back to him so he could offer further service to the aging apostle.

Out of that dilemma comes this little masterpiece — a classic example of skill in motivation. As the comments show, Paul weaves his argument with great expertise, as he persuades Philemon to treat his returned slave with Christian love. He does not hurry his argument, but carefully lays each piece in place so that the actual request (v. 17) rests upon a solid foundation. Even then he goes further in giving Philemon a "promissory note" (v. 19), guaranteeing that any loss, should Philemon insist, would be repaid.

It is assumed Philemon respected Paul's wishes, and this is a reason the letter has been preserved. In the letter from Ignatius of Antioch to the church in Ephesus (early second century) he speaks of an Onesimus who was bishop of that church. Some suppose this was the former slave, and the conjecture, though not provable, is not impossible. If it is true the influence of Onesimus may have played an important part in the preservation of the letter.

Readers of Acts and of Paul's other letters know the apostle could be quite forthright when necessary. This trait may have been responsible for the opposition aroused against him, both from without and within the church. But he was also a man of sensitivity and tact, as this letter shows. Thus the epistle is a much needed instruction in ways Christians might act in their relations with one another. It gives us a case study of just what love should do in a specific instance.

Though the influence of Christianity penetrated Mediterranean culture in powerful ways (see Acts 19:26f), the New Testament does not show us Christian efforts to create large scale social change by legal and other means. Since the return of Christ was prominent in their minds, and expected by many to occur soon, that event would be the time for the rectification of injustices. But the principles taught by Jesus powerfully altered relationships. Thus though Paul does not denounce slavery generally, he sets forth standards of conduct which would eliminate cruelty and unkind domination. They also enhance the recognition that all men are before all else under God, and thus no man has complete ownership of another. If allowed a fuller influence in society, these principles would be truly transforming. But this would be by consent, not by coercion. One wonders how even today's world would be changed were the leaven of Christianity allowed to have its full impact?

OUTLINE

INTRODUCTION — 1-3

I. PRAYER AND COMMENDATION — 4-7

II. THE REQUEST — 18-20

    A. Paul's Appeal of Love — 8-11

    B. Onesimus Sent Back — 12-16

    C. Welcome Him as You Would Me — 17-20

    CONCLUSION — 21-25

BIBLIOGRAPHY
PHILEMON

Bruce, F.F. *The Epistles to the Colossians, to Philemon, and to the Ephesians*. Grand Rapids: Eerdmans, 1984.

Lohse, Eduard. *Colossians and Philemon*. Philadelphia: Fortress, 1971.

Melick, Richard. *Philippians, Colossians, Philemon*. Nashville: Broadman, 1991.

O'Brien, Peter. *Colossians, Philemon*. Waco, TX: Word Books, 1982.

Patzia, Arthur. *Ephesians, Colossians, Philemon*. Peabody, MA: Hendrickson, 1984.

Weed, Michael. *The Letters of Paul to the Ephesians, Colossians, and Philemon*. Austin: Sweet, 1971.

PHILEMON

INTRODUCTION (1-3)

¹Paul, a prisoner of Christ Jesus, and Timothy our brother, To Philemon our dear friend and fellow worker, ²to Apphia our sister, to Archippus our fellow soldier and to the church that meets in your home: ³Grace to you and peace from God our Father and the Lord Jesus Christ.

Paul uses the usual letter form in writing Philemon. Cf. notes at Philippians 1:1.

V. 1 Paul, a prisoner of Christ Jesus,

Verses 1 and 2 mention five persons, and each name is accompanied with a description. Paul was a prisoner, a fact which he notes also in verses 9, 10, 13, and 23. This was a literal incarceration (as in Eph 3:1; 4:1; 2 Tim 1:8), though there are contexts where Paul's description of himself as Christ's slave has led some to conclude imprisonment meant he was Christ's captive (see Rom 6:22; 1 Cor 7:22; Phil 1:1).

Paul may have been doing no more than describing his situation. But could Philemon, as he read, have been called to personal sacrifice by Paul's example of his own loss of freedom for Christ's sake? As Paul's dedication has inspired Christians through the ages, so might it have inspired Philemon.

Paul chose not to call himself an apostle, likely because that term might have implied an authority which he did not wish to stress in his dealings with Philemon.

237

and Timothy our brother,

On the significance of Timothy's name, see the discussion at Philippians 1:1. That he is noted here and not with the names in verses 23f could indicate that he played a more significant role as Paul's helper than did the others. If Philemon had been converted while Paul was in Ephesus on his third tour, he may have been acquainted with Timothy (cf. Acts 18:5; 19:22). If Timothy was known to Philemon, it seems inconceivable that Paul would not have mentioned him.

To Philemon our dear friend and fellow worker,

Nothing is known of Philemon besides what this letter reveals. The context indicates he alone was the one to whom Paul's concerns were directed, though any decision he made would involve his family to some extent. It is likely true, given his position as a slave owner and probably as owner of a house in which Christians met, that he was a man of some substance. "Dear friend" (ἀγαπητός, *agapētos*) shows Paul's affection for him (some translations have "beloved") and introduces a Greek term which is woven throughout the letter ("love" in 5,7,9, and "dear" in 16). Paul's relation to Philemon was couched in love, as all Christians are immersed in God's love. Given such a marvelous context, it is easy to see the power of Paul's appeal.

"Fellow worker" is also used to describe the persons mentioned in verses 23f. Perhaps Philemon had once been Paul's personal helper, but more likely the term indicates his involvement in God's work in a broader sense.

V. 2 to Apphia our sister,

Two individuals and a group are now added to the addressees. Apphia obviously bore a special relation to Philemon to be thus addressed. Most think she was his wife, though it has also been suggested that she was a sister in the flesh. However, "sister" probably indicates she was a Christian.

to Archippus our fellow soldier

Archippus was addressed in somewhat mysterious terms in

Colossians 4:17 (see notes there). The most common assumption is that he was the son of Philemon and Apphia. John Knox, however, has advanced the novel theory that Archippus was the leader of the church in Colosse, while Philemon led the church in the entire area. On this view Paul wrote Philemon and Apphia to seek their aid in influencing Archippus, who was the master of Onesimus. This theory has been vigorously attacked and rejected by the bulk of the scholarly world. "Fellow soldier" also described Epaphroditus in Philippians 2:25 (see notes there). The term is one Paul used for himself and for those who assisted in his labors or stood beside him in special ways. Archippus may have had special responsibilities in the church at Colosse.

and to the church that meets in your home:

It is generally assumed a church met in Philemon's home. Other references to house churches are found in Romans 16:5; 1 Corinthians 16:19; and Colossians 4:15. Occasionally it has been suggested this was the home of Archippus, since "your" is singular, and Archippus' name is nearest to "home."

More controversial is whether the letter was intended to be read to the whole church, or whether only greetings were to be given the church. Commentators argue the case both ways. Would a private letter be read publicly? On the other hand the moral suasion of the church could encourage Philemon. But would Paul intend that kind of pressure on his friend? Would Philemon, receiving the letter, wish it made public? Would he wish for the prayers and wisdom of the church? Were Paul's letters customarily read publicly, even when addressed to individuals? Or did Paul write many such personal letters, now lost to us, which were never intended for public reading?

V. 3 Grace to you and peace from God our Father and the Lord Jesus Christ.

This greeting, traditional in form, is basically the same as in Philippians 1:2 and Colossians 1:2 (see also Eph 1:2). See the notes on those passages. The entire community was greeted, but this does not prove or disprove that the letter was to be read to all. A broader address is found in verses twenty-three and twenty-four. One might ask, in addition, how "grace" and "peace" figure in the message of this letter.

I. PRAYER AND COMMENDATION (4-7)

[4]I always thank my God as I remember you in my prayers, [5]because I hear about your faith in the Lord Jesus and your love for all the saints. [6]I pray that you may be active in sharing your faith, so that you will have a full understanding of every good thing we have in Christ. [7]Your love has given me great joy and encouragement, because you, brother, have refreshed the hearts of the saints.

This section follows the usual Hellenistic letter form. Verses 4-6 are the thanks and the prayer, while verse 7 moves to the body of the letter. As was generally the case this paragraph places ideas before the reader to which later sentences will refer. Note prayer (vv. 4,22), love (vv. 5,7,9), fellowship (vv. 6,17), good (vv. 6,14), heart (vv. 7,12,20), refresh (vv. 7,20), and brother (vv. 7,20). Paul makes his way into his main argument with great skill. Cf. with this passage Colossians 1:3-14.

V. 4 I always thank my God as I remember you in my prayers,
Paul now speaks alone, indicating a regular regimen of prayer ("always") for his brother. His thanks hints that nothing bad had been said about Philemon by Onesimus — or at least nothing that had influenced Paul negatively. There may also be the intimation that Paul was praying that Philemon would do what he requested. Further content of the prayer is not given until verse 6.

V. 5 because I hear about your faith in the Lord Jesus and your love for all the saints.
The reason for Paul's thanks is now given. The singular

pronouns ("your") indicate it was Philemon alone whom he was complimenting. The NIV departs from a literal rendering of the Greek, which would read ". . . love and faith . . . in . . . Jesus and to all the saints." Some argue that both qualities (love, faith) are to be understood as being directed to both "objects" (Jesus, saints). The NIV, however, in concert with most modern interpreters, sees the text differently. Those holding this view note that one would not have "faith" in the saints; rather "faithfulness" would be the appropriate term. They argue the structure is chiastic (cf. Col 1:4), thus faith in Jesus (the first and last elements) go together, as do love for the saints (second and third elements). Further, verse 6 speaks of faith in relation to Christ, and verse 7 of love for the saints, offering a parallel to this reading. Discussion of these details, though significant for full understanding, should not draw attention away from the splendid character of the one thus complimented. These qualities boded well for a positive response to the request Paul would make in verses 17 and 18 (and see v. 22).

V. 6 I pray that you may be active in sharing your faith, so that you will have a full understanding of every good thing we have in Christ.

Now Paul's specific prayer is described. The NIV adds "I pray," which is not in the Greek, to convey this. This verse is an interpretive mare's nest. Yet the variant possibilities do not involve large matters of doctrine, but more subtle differences in meaning. Patzia offers a literal translation of the Greek as follows: "so as the fellowship [NIV 'sharing'] of your faith working [NIV 'active'] may become in full knowledge [NIV 'understanding'] every good thing in us for Christ."[1] Comparison of English translations demonstrates the problems inherent in rendering these words into meaningful English. As we interpret the passage, we should keep in mind Paul's purpose

---

[1]Arthur Patzia, *Ephesians, Colossians, Philemon* (Peabody, MA: Hendrickson, 1984), p. 109.

to influence Philemon to adopt appropriate behavior toward Onesimus.

Melick, relying in part on O'Brien, offers a helpful analysis of the interpretive difficulties involved.[2] First, what is meant by "sharing" (κοινωνία, *koinōnia*) faith? A whole spate of suggestions have been made by scholars over the years (see discussions in Melick and O'Brien). The NIV could be taken to imply a prayer for evangelistic activity, but that was not Paul's interest in this epistle. We believe the reference was to the remarkable fellowship binding those with a common faith in Christ (weeping and rejoicing together) that would lead Philemon to welcome Onesimus. On this view, for Philemon to refuse Paul's request would be to work against Paul's prayers.

Second in Melick's list is determining the meaning of "in Christ." The expression is unusual, since in place of the usual "in" (ἐν, *en*) Paul used "into" (εἰς, *eis*). O'Brien argues, however, that the difference is only stylistic, to avoid a third use of *en* in the verse, and thus *eis* means the same thing as *en*.[3] Paul may be saying that those who understand life in Christ would wish to act generously and lovingly. Perhaps the expression would lead Philemon to ask how Christ would have dealt with the Onesimus situation. Both the nature of Christ and the blessing of incorporation into his body may be implied here.

Third, how are we to understand "active," "good thing," and "understanding" in relation to Christ? O'Brien argues "effective" is a better translation than "active," since Paul had already been active.[4] Paul wished to channel his energy in a new direction. He was saying that enhanced understanding would lead to this. "Understanding" was probably not just cognitive, but would be experiential. One knows what being in Christ means by living the life. "Every good thing" would certainly imply God's forgiveness. If so, it would set an attitude in

---

[2]Richard Melick, *Philippians, Colossians, Philemon* (Nashville: Broadman, 1991), pp. 353-355.

[3]Peter O'Brien, *Colossians, Philemon* (Waco, TX: Word Books, 1982), p. 281.

[4]Ibid., p. 280.

the mind of Philemon which would lead to acceptance of Paul's later request.

Fortunately we may conclude that Philemon, knowing his context as we cannot, would understand Paul's words more exactly than is allowed us by our distance from the original circumstances.

V. 7 Your love has given me great joy and encouragement,

This verse transitions from the prayer toward the body of the letter. Though the reference to love specifically echoes verse 5, what Paul says here rests on the foundation of verses 4-6. Later Paul would appeal on the basis of love (v. 9). This quality in Philemon had benefitted Paul, refreshed the saints, and formed a solid reason why Paul's later request would be granted. Paul's magnanimity of spirit is shown in his joy that others were helped (cf. Rom 12:9-13; 2 Cor 11:29). He hoped this help would extend to another saint — Onesimus.

because you, brother, have refreshed the hearts of the saints.

We do not know if Paul contemplated a specific deed of Philemon or if he was speaking in general terms about a constant trait. "Hearts" translates a word (σπλάγχνα, *splanchna*) that describes the seat of the emotions (cf. the same word in vv. 12,20), perhaps implying that Philemon's refreshment provided emotional uplift.

II. THE REQUEST (8-20)

A. PAUL'S APPEAL OF LOVE (8-11)

[8]**Therefore, although in Christ I could be bold and order you to do what you ought to do,** [9]**yet I appeal to you on the basis of love. I then, as Paul — an old man and now also a prisoner of Christ Jesus —** [10]**I appeal to you for my son Onesimus,**[a] **who became my son while I was in chains.** [11]**Formerly he was useless to you, but now he has become useful both to you and to me.**

[a]*10 Onesimus* means *useful.*

Now Paul comes to the central concern of his letter. He begins by discussing motivation. The moving force for Philemon's action, an action as yet unspecified, was to be love, rather than response to a mandate. In verses 8-16 Paul describes the situation with which he was concerned, but does not make his specific request until verse 17. He tiptoes his way to the point.

Though the NIV divides the text 8-11 and 12-16, in the Greek verses 8-14 are one sentence.

V. 8 Therefore, although in Christ I could be bold and order you to do what you ought to do,

In this verse Paul eschewed the use of command. Obedience to a command may be done because of a recognition of authority, but it does not always come from a willing heart. Paul wanted Philemon to respond because Philemon saw it as the right thing to do. Thus the following verses would deal with various reasons for that response. Though not given in the form of "thou shalt," when considered in light of Christian ethics those reasons were virtually irresistible. It would seem Paul knew Philemon would do as he was asked to do, but he pays him the compliment of indicating he knows it would be done from the proper Christian motives, not from coercion.

If Philemon had refused, would Paul then have resorted to an apostolic demand? We do not think Paul was saying or implying "do it for the following reasons, but if you don't I must require it." We believe he had no doubt of Philemon's response.

Paul's boldness may have been due to the intimacy of his relation to Philemon, or, more likely, because of their common faith ("in Christ"). Nothing in these words implies the imposition of apostolic authority. Rather it was the working out of the way life is lived in Christ. Apostolic authority, at its most basic level, would still rest upon the lifestyle and teachings of Jesus. If Philemon were unwilling to act for the reasons Paul gave, it is doubtful whether the imposition of an apostle's weight would have changed him.